Bird *by* Bird

Some Instructions
on Writing and Life

Anne Lamott

ANCHOR BOOKS
A DIVISION OF RANDOM HOUSE, INC.
NEW YORK

First Anchor Books Edition, October 1995

Copyright © 1994 by Anne Lamott

All rights reserved under International and Pan-American Copyright
Conventions. Published in the United States by Anchor Books, a division of
Random House, Inc., New York, and simultaneously in Canada by Random
House of Canada Limited, Toronto. Originally published in hardcover in the
United States by Pantheon Books in 1994. This edition published by
arrangement with Pantheon Books.

Anchor Books and colophon are registered trademarks
of Random House, Inc.

Permissions acknowledgments appear on p. 238.

Library of Congress Cataloging-in-Publication Data

Lamott, Anne.
    Bird by bird : some instructions on writing and life / Anne
Lamott.—1st Anchor Books ed.
      p.   cm.
    Originally published : New York : Pantheon Books, 1994.
    1. Authorship—Handbooks, manuals, etc.   I. Title.
PN147.L315   1995
808′.02—dc20   95-10225
                                              CIP

Book design by Jan Melchior

www.anchorbooks.com

Printed in the United States of America
30 29 28 27 26 25

Bird by Bird

ALSO BY ANNE LAMOTT

Hard Laughter

Rosie

Joe Jones

All New People

Operating Instructions

Crooked Little Heart

Traveling Mercies

*This book is dedicated
to Don Carpenter*

& Neshama Franklin

& John Kaye

Contents

Acknowledgments

I would like to acknowledge the extraordinary debt I owe to the writers who have told me such wise things about writing over the years: Martin Cruz Smith, Jane Vandenburgh, Ethan Canin, Alice Adams, Dennis McFarland, Orville Schell, and Tom Weston.

I would not be able to get my work done without the continual support and vision of my editor, Jack Shoemaker. My agent, Chuck Verrill, is just wonderful as is Nancy Palmer Jones, who copy-edited this book (and the last) with enormous skill and warmth and precision.

I want to mention once again that I do not think I'd even be alive today if not for the people of St. Andrew Presbyterian Church, Marin City, California.

Sam said to me the other day, "I love you like 20 tyrannosauruses on 20 mountaintops," and this is the exact same way in which I love him.

Introduction

I grew up around a father and a mother who read every chance they got, who took us to the library every Thursday night to load up on books for the coming week. Most nights after dinner my father stretched out on the couch to read, while my mother sat with her book in the easy chair and the three of us kids each retired to our own private reading stations. Our house was very quiet after dinner—unless, that is, some of my father's writer friends were over. My father was a writer, as were most of the men with whom he hung out. They were not the quietest people on earth, but they were mostly very masculine and kind. Usually in the afternoons, when that day's work was done, they hung out at the no name bar in Sausalito, but sometimes they came to our house for drinks and ended up staying for supper. I loved them, but every so often one of them would pass out at the dinner table. I was an anxious child to begin with, and I found this unnerving.

Every morning, no matter how late he had been up, my father rose at 5:30, went to his study, wrote for a couple of hours, made us all breakfast, read the paper with my mother, and then went back to work for the rest of the morning. Many years passed before I realized that he did this by choice, for a living, and that he was not unemployed or mentally ill. I wanted him to have a regular job where he put on a necktie and went off somewhere with the other fathers and sat in a little office and smoked. But the idea of spending entire days in someone else's office doing someone else's work did not suit my father's soul. I think it would have killed him. He did end up dying rather early, in his mid-fifties, but at least he had lived on his own terms.

So I grew up around this man who sat at his desk in the study all day and wrote books and articles about the places and people he had seen and known. He read a lot of poetry. Sometimes he traveled. He could go anyplace he wanted with a sense of purpose. One of the gifts of being a writer is that it gives you an excuse to do things, to go places and explore. Another is that writing motivates you to look closely at life, at life as it lurches by and tramps around.

Writing taught my father to pay attention; my father in turn taught other people to pay attention and then to write down their thoughts and observations. His students were the prisoners at San Quentin who took part in the creative-writing program. But he taught me, too, mostly by example. He taught the prisoners and me to put a little bit down on paper every day, and to read all the great books and plays we could get our hands on. He taught us to read poetry. He taught us to be bold and original and to let ourselves make mistakes, and that Thurber was right when he said, "You might as well fall flat on your face as lean over too far backwards." But while he helped the prisoners and me to discover that we had a lot of feelings and observations and memories and dreams and (God knows) opinions we wanted to share, we all ended up just the tiniest bit resentful when we found the one fly in the ointment: that at some point we had to actually sit down and write.

I believe writing was easier for me than for the prisoners because I was still a child. But I always found it hard. I started writing when I was seven or eight. I was very shy and strange-looking, loved reading above everything else, weighed about forty pounds at the time, and was so tense that I walked around with my shoulders up to my ears, like Richard Nixon. I saw a home movie once of a birthday party I went to in the first grade, with all these cute little boys and girls playing together like puppies, and all of a sudden I scuttled across the screen like Prufrock's crab. I was very clearly the one who was going to grow up to be a serial killer, or keep dozens and dozens of cats. Instead, I got funny. I got funny because boys, older boys I didn't even know, would ride by on their bicycles and taunt me about my weird looks. Each time felt like a drive-by shooting. I think this is why I walked like Nixon: I think I was trying to plug my ears with my shoulders, but they wouldn't quite reach. So first I got funny and then I started to write, although I did not always write funny things.

The first poem I wrote that got any attention was about John Glenn. The first stanza went, "Colonel John Glenn went up to heaven / in his spaceship, *Friendship Seven.*" There were many, many verses. It was like one of the old English ballads my mother taught us to sing while she played the piano. Each song had thirty or forty verses, which would leave my male relatives flattened to our couches and armchairs as if by centrifugal force, staring unblinking up at the ceiling.

The teacher read the John Glenn poem to my second-grade class. It was a great moment; the other children looked at me as though I had learned to drive. It turned out that the teacher had submitted the poem to a California state schools competition, and it had won some sort of award. It appeared in a mimeographed collection. I understood immediately the thrill of seeing oneself in print. It provides some sort of primal verification: you are in print; therefore you exist. Who knows what this urge is all about, to appear somewhere outside yourself, instead of feeling stuck inside your muddled but stroboscopic mind, peering out like a little undersea animal—a spiny blenny, for instance—from inside your tiny cave? Seeing yourself in print is such an amazing concept: you can get so much attention without having to actually show up somewhere. While others who have something to say or who want to be effectual, like musicians or baseball players or politicians, have to get out there in front of people, writers, who tend to be shy, get to stay home and still be public. There are many obvious advantages to this. You don't have to dress up, for instance, and you can't hear them boo you right away.

Sometimes I got to sit on the floor of my father's study and write my poems while he sat at his desk writing his books. Every couple of years, another book of his was published. Books were revered in our house, and great writers admired above everyone else. Special books got displayed prominently: on the coffee table, on the radio, on the back of the john. I grew up reading the blurbs on dust jackets and the reviews of my father's books in the papers. All of this made me start wanting to be a writer when I grew up—to be artistic, a free spirit, and yet also to be the rare working-class person in charge of her own life.

Still, I worried that there was never quite enough money at our house. I worried that my father was going to turn into a bum like some of his writer friends. I remember when I was ten years old, my father published a piece in a magazine that mentioned his having spent an afternoon on a porch at Stinson Beach with a bunch of other writers and that they had all been drinking lots of red wine and smoking marijuana. No one smoked marijuana in those days except jazz musicians, and they were all also heroin addicts. Nice white middle-class fathers were not supposed to be smoking marijuana; they were supposed to be sailing or playing tennis. My friends' fathers, who were teachers and doctors and fire fighters and lawyers, did not smoke marijuana. Most of them didn't even drink, and they certainly did not have colleagues who came over and passed out at the table over the tuna casserole. Reading my father's article, I could only imagine that the world was breaking down, that the next time I burst into my dad's study to show him my report card he'd be crouched under the desk, with one of my mother's nylon stockings knotted around his upper arm, looking up at me like a cornered wolf. I felt that this was going to be a problem; I was sure that we would be ostracized in our community.

All I ever wanted was to belong, to wear that hat of belonging.

In seventh and eighth grades I still weighed about forty pounds. I was twelve years old and had been getting teased about my strange looks for most of my life. This is a difficult country to look too different in—the United States of Advertising, as Paul Krassner puts it—and if you are too skinny or too tall or dark or weird or short or frizzy or homely or poor or nearsighted, you get crucified. I did.

But I was funny. So the popular kids let me hang out with them, go to their parties, and watch them neck with each other. This, as you might imagine, did not help my self-esteem a great deal. I thought I was a total loser. But one day I took a notebook and a pen when I went to Bolinas Beach with my father (who was not, as far as I could tell, shooting drugs yet). With the writer's equivalent of canvas and brush, I wrote a description of what I saw: "I walked to the lip of the water and let the foamy tongue of the rushing liquid lick my toes. A sand crab burrowed a hole a few inches from my foot and then disappeared into the damp sand. . . ." I will spare you the rest. It goes on for quite a while. My father convinced me to show it to a teacher, and it ended up being included in a real textbook. This deeply impressed my teachers and parents and a few kids, even some of the popular kids, who invited me to more parties so I could watch them all make out even more frequently.

One of the popular girls came home with me after school one day, to spend the night. We found my parents rejoicing over the arrival of my dad's new novel, the first copy off the press. We were all so thrilled and proud, and this girl seemed to think I had the coolest possible father: a writer. (Her father sold cars.) We went out to dinner, where we all toasted one another. Things in the family just couldn't have been better, and here was a friend to witness it.

Then that night, before we went to sleep, I picked up the new novel and began to read the first page to my friend. We were lying side by side in sleeping bags on my floor. The first page turned out to be about a man and a woman in bed together, having sex. The man was playing with the woman's nipple. I began to giggle with mounting hysteria. Oh, this is great, I thought, beaming jocularly at my friend. I covered my mouth with one hand, like a blushing Charlie Chaplin, and pantomimed that I was about to toss that silly book over my shoulder. This is wonderful, I thought, throwing back my head to laugh jovially; my father writes pornography.

In the dark, I glowed like a light bulb with shame. You could have read by me. I never mentioned the book to my father, although over the next couple of years, I went through it late at night, looking for more sexy parts, of which there were a number. It was very confusing. It made me feel very scared and sad.

Then a strange thing happened. My father wrote an article for a magazine, called "A Lousy Place to Raise Kids," and it was about Marin County and specifically the community where we lived, which is as beautiful a place as one can imagine. Yet the people on our peninsula were second only to the Native Americans in the slums of Oakland in the rate of alcoholism, and the drug abuse among teenagers was, as my father wrote, soul chilling, and there was rampant divorce and mental breakdown and wayward sexual behavior. My father wrote disparagingly about the men in the community, their values and materialistic frenzy, and about their wives, "these estimable women, the wives of doctors, architects, and lawyers, in tennis dresses and cotton frocks, tanned and well preserved, wandering the aisles of our supermarkets with glints of madness in their eyes." No one in our town came off looking great. "This is the great tragedy of California," he wrote in the last paragraph, "for a life oriented to leisure is in the end a life oriented to death—the greatest leisure of all."

There was just one problem: I was an avid tennis player. The tennis ladies were my friends. I practiced every afternoon at the same tennis club as they; I sat with them on the weekends and waited for the men (who had priority) to be done so we could get on the courts. And now my father had made them look like decadent zombies.

I thought we were ruined. But my older brother came home from school that week with a photocopy of my father's article that his teachers in both social studies and English had passed out to their classes; John was a hero to his classmates. There was an enormous response in the community: in the next few months I was snubbed by a number of men and women at the tennis club, but at the same time, people stopped my father on the street when we were walking together, and took his hand in both of theirs, as if he had done them some personal favor. Later that summer I came to know how they felt, when I read *Catcher in the Rye* for the first time and knew what it was like to have someone speak for me, to close a book with a sense of both triumph and relief, one lonely isolated social animal finally making contact.

I started writing a lot in high school: journals, impassioned antiwar pieces, parodies of the writers I loved. And I began to notice something important. The other kids always wanted me to tell them stories of what had happened, even—or especially—when they had been there. Parties that got away from us, blowups in the classroom or on the school yard, scenes involving their parents that we had witnessed—I could make the story happen. I could make it vivid and funny, and even exaggerate some of it so that the event became almost mythical, and the people involved seemed larger, and there was a sense of larger significance, of meaning.

I'm sure my father was the person on whom his friends relied to tell their stories, in school and college. I know for sure that he was later, in the town where he was raising his children. He could take major events or small episodes from daily life and shade or exaggerate things in such a way as to capture their shape and substance, capture what life felt like in the society in which he and his friends lived and worked and bred. People looked to him to put into words what was going on.

I suspect that he was a child who thought differently than his peers, who may have had serious conversations with grownups, who as a young person, like me, accepted being alone quite a lot. I think that this sort of person often becomes either a writer or a career criminal. Throughout my childhood I believed that what I thought about was different from what other kids thought about. It was not necessarily more profound, but there was a struggle going on inside me to find some sort of creative or spiritual or aesthetic way of seeing the world and organizing it in my head. I read more than other kids; I luxuriated in books. Books were my refuge. I sat in corners with my little finger hooked over my bottom lip, reading, in a trance, lost in the places and times to which books took me. And there was a moment during my junior year in high school when I began to believe that I could do what other writers were doing. I came to believe that I might be able to put a pencil in my hand and make something magical happen.

Then I wrote some terrible, terrible stories.

In college the whole world opened up, and the books and poets being taught in my English and philosophy classes gave me the feeling for the first time in my life that there was hope, hope that I might find my place in a community. I felt that in my strange new friends and in certain new books, I was meeting my other half. Some people wanted to get rich or famous, but my friends and I wanted to get real. We wanted to get deep. (Also, I suppose, we wanted to get laid.) I devoured books like a person taking vitamins, afraid that otherwise I would remain this gelatinous narcissist, with no possibility of ever becoming thoughtful, of ever being taken seriously. I became a socialist, for five weeks. Then the bus ride to my socialist meetings wore me out. I was drawn to oddballs, ethnic people, theater people, poets, radicals, gays and lesbians—and somehow they all helped me become some of those things I wanted so desperately to become: political, intellectual, artistic.

My friends turned me on to Kierkegaard, Beckett, Doris Lessing. I swooned with the excitement and nourishment of it all. I remember reading C. S. Lewis for the first time, *Surprised by Joy,* and how, looking inside himself, he found "a zoo of lusts, a bedlam of ambitions, a nursery of fears, a harem of fondled hatreds." I felt elated and absolved. I had thought that the people one admired, the kind, smart people of the world, were not like that on the inside, were different from me and, say, Toulouse-Lautrec.

I started writing sophomoric articles for the college paper. Luckily, I was a sophomore. I was incompetent in all college ways except one—I got the best grades in English. I wrote the best papers. But I was ambitious; I wanted to be recognized on a larger scale. So I dropped out at nineteen to become a famous writer.

I moved back to San Francisco and became a famous Kelly Girl instead. I was famous for my incompetence and weepiness.

I wept with boredom and disbelief. Then I landed a job as a clerk-typist at a huge engineering and construction firm in the city, in the nuclear quality-assurance department, where I labored under a tsunami wave of triplicate forms and memos. It was very upsetting. It was also so boring that it made my eyes feel ringed with dark circles, like Lurch. I finally figured out that most of this paperwork could be tossed without there being any real . . . well . . . fallout, and this freed me up to write short stories instead.

"Do it every day for a while," my father kept saying. "Do it as you would do scales on the piano. Do it by prearrangement with yourself. Do it as a debt of honor. And make a commitment to finishing things."

So in addition to writing furtively at the office, I wrote every night for an hour or more, often in coffeehouses with a notepad and my pen, drinking great quantities of wine because this is what writers do; this was what my father and all his friends did. It worked for them, although there was now a new and disturbing trend—they had started committing suicide. This was very painful for my father, of course. But we both kept writing.

I eventually moved out to Bolinas, where my father and younger brother had moved the year before when my parents split up. I began to teach tennis and clean houses for a living. Every day for a couple of years I wrote little snippets and vignettes, but mainly I concentrated on my magnum opus, a short story called "Arnold." A bald, bearded psychiatrist named Arnold is hanging out one day with a slightly depressed young female writer and her slightly depressed younger brother. Arnold gives them all sorts of helpful psychological advice but then, at the end, gives up, gets down on his haunches, and waddles around quacking like a duck to amuse them. This is a theme I have always loved, where a couple of totally hopeless cases run into someone, like a clown or a foreigner, who gives them a little spin for a while and who says in effect, "I'm lost, too! But look—I know how to catch rabbits!"

It was a terrible story.

I wrote a lot of other things, too. I took notes on the people around me, in my town, in my family, in my memory. I took notes on my own state of mind, my grandiosity, the low self-esteem. I wrote down the funny stuff I overheard. I learned to be like a ship's rat, veined ears trembling, and I learned to scribble it all down.

But mostly I worked on my short story "Arnold." Every few months I would send it to my father's agent in New York, Elizabeth McKee.

"Well," she'd write back, "it's really coming along now."

I did this for several years. I wanted to be published so badly. I heard a preacher say recently that hope is a revolutionary patience; let me add that so is being a writer. Hope begins in the dark, the stubborn hope that if you just show up and try to do the right thing, the dawn will come. You wait and watch and work: you don't give up.

I didn't give up, largely because of my father's faith in me. And then, unfortunately, when I was twenty-three, I suddenly had a story to tell. My father was diagnosed with brain cancer. He and my brothers and I were devastated, but somehow we managed, just barely, to keep our heads above water. My father told me to pay attention and to take notes. "You tell your version," he said, "and I am going to tell mine."

I began to write about what my father was going through, and then began to shape these writings into connected short stories. I wove in all the vignettes and snippets I'd been working on in the year before Dad's diagnosis, and came up with five chapters that sort of hung together. My father, who was too sick to write his own rendition, loved them, and had me ship them off to Elizabeth, our agent. And then I waited and waited and waited, growing old and withered in the course of a month. But I think she must have read them in a state of near euphoria, thrilled to find herself not reading "Arnold." She is not a religious woman by any stretch, but I always picture her clutching those stories to her chest, eyes closed, swaying slightly, moaning, "Thank ya, Lord."

So she sent them around New York, and Viking made us an offer. And thus the process began. The book came out when I was twenty-six, when my father had been dead for a year. God! I had a book published! It was everything I had ever dreamed of. And I had reached nirvana, right? Well.

I believed, before I sold my first book, that publication would be instantly and automatically gratifying, an affirming and romantic experience, a Hallmark commercial where one runs and leaps in slow motion across a meadow filled with wildflowers into the arms of acclaim and self-esteem.

This did not happen for me.

The months before a book comes out of the chute are, for most writers, right up there with the worst life has to offer, pretty much like the first twenty minutes of *Apocalypse Now,* with Martin Sheen in the motel room in Saigon, totally decompensating. The waiting and the fantasies, both happy and grim, wear you down. Plus there is the matter of the early reviews that come out about two months before publication. The first two notices I got on this tender book I'd written about my dying, now dead father said that my book was a total waste of time, a boring, sentimental, self-indulgent sack of spider puke.

This is not verbatim.

I was a little edgy for the next six weeks, as you can imagine. I had lots and lots of drinks every night, and told lots of strangers at the bar about how my dad had died and I'd written this book about it, and how the early reviewers had criticized it, and then I'd start to cry and need a few more drinks, and then I'd end up telling them about this great dog we'd had named Llewelyn who had to be put to sleep when I was twelve, which still made me so sad even to think about, I'd tell my audience, that it was all I could do not to go into the rest room and blow my brains out.

Then the book came out. I got some terrific reviews in important places, and a few bad ones. There were a few book-signing parties, a few interviews, and a number of important people claimed to love it. But overall it seemed that I was not in fact going to be taking early retirement. I had secretly believed that trumpets would blare, major reviewers would proclaim that not since *Moby Dick* had an American novel so captured life in all of its dizzying complexity. And this is what I thought when my second book came out, and my third, and my fourth, and my fifth. And each time I was wrong.

But I still encourage anyone who feels at all compelled to write to do so. I just try to warn people who hope to get published that publication is not all that it is cracked up to be. But writing is. Writing has so much to give, so much to teach, so many surprises. That thing you had to force yourself to do—the actual act of writing—turns out to be the best part. It's like discovering that while you thought you needed the tea ceremony for the caffeine, what you really needed was the tea ceremony. The act of writing turns out to be its own reward.

I've managed to get some work done nearly every day of my adult life, without impressive financial success. Yet I would do it all over again in a hot second, mistakes and doldrums and breakdowns and all. Sometimes I could not tell you exactly why, especially when it feels pointless and pitiful, like Sisyphus with cash-flow problems. Other days, though, my writing is like a person to me—the person who, after all these years, still makes sense to me. It reminds me of "The Wild Rose," a poem Wendell Berry wrote for his wife:

Sometimes hidden from me
in daily custom and in trust,

so that I live by you unaware
as by the beating of my heart,

Suddenly you flare in my sight,
a wild rose blooming at the edge
of thicket, grace and light
where yesterday was only shade,

and once again I am blessed, choosing
again what I chose before.

Ever since I was a little kid, I've thought that there was something noble and mysterious about writing, about the people who could do it well, who could create a world as if they were little gods or sorcerers. All my life I've felt that there was something magical about people who could get into other people's minds and skin, who could take people like me out of ourselves and then take us back to ourselves. And you know what? I still do.

So now I teach. This just sort of happened. Someone offered me a gig teaching a writing workshop about ten years ago, and I've been teaching writing classes ever since. But you can't *teach* writing, people tell me. And I say, 'Who the hell are you, God's dean of admissions?"

If people show up in one of my classes and want to learn to write, or to write better, I can tell them everything that has helped me along the way and what it is like for me on a daily basis. I can teach them little things that may not be in any of the great books on writing. For instance, I'm not sure if anyone else has mentioned that December is traditionally a bad month for writing. It is a month of Mondays. Mondays are not good writing days. One has had all that freedom over the weekend, all that authenticity, all those dreamy dreams, and then your angry mute Slavic Uncle Monday arrives, and it is time to sit down at your desk. So I would simply recommend to the people in my workshops that they never start a large writing project on any Monday in December. Why set yourself up for failure?

Interviewers ask famous writers why they write, and it was (if I remember correctly) the poet John Ashbery who answered, "Because I want to." Flannery O'Connor answered, "Because I'm good at it," and when the occasional interviewer asks me, I quote them both. Then I add that other than writing, I am completely unemployable. But really, secretly, when I'm not being smart-alecky, it's because I want to and I'm good at it. I always mention a scene from the movie *Chariots of Fire* in which, as I remember it, the Scottish runner, Eric Liddell, who is the hero, is walking along with his missionary sister on a gorgeous heathery hillside in Scotland. She is nagging him to give up training for the Olympics and to get back to doing his missionary work at their church's mission in China. And he replies that he wants to go to China because he feels it is God's will for him, but that first he is going to train with all of his heart, because God also made him very, very fast.

So God made some of us fast in this area of working with

words, and he gave us the gift of loving to read with the same kind of passion with which we love nature. My students at the writing workshops have this gift of loving to read, and some of them are really fast, really good with words, and some of them aren't really fast and don't write all that well, but they still love good writing, and they just want to write. And I say, "Hey! That is good enough for me. Come on *down*."

So I tell them what it will be like for me at the desk the next morning when I sit down to work, with a few ideas and a lot of blank paper, with hideous conceit and low self-esteem in equal measure, fingers poised on the keyboard. I tell them they'll want to be really good right off, and they may not be, but they *might* be good someday if they just keep the faith and keep practicing. And they may even go from wanting to have written something to just wanting to be writing, wanting to be working on something, like they'd want to be playing the piano or tennis, because writing brings with it so much joy, so much challenge. It is work and play together. When they are working on their books or stories, their heads will spin with ideas and invention. They'll see the world through new eyes. Everything they see and hear and learn will become grist for the mill. At cocktail parties or in line at the post office, they will be gleaning small moments and overheard expressions: they'll sneak away to scribble these things down. They will have days at the desk of frantic boredom, of angry hopelessness, of wanting to quit forever, and there will be days when it feels like they have caught and are riding a wave.

And then I tell my students that the odds of their getting

published and of it bringing them financial security, peace of mind, and even joy are probably not that great. Ruin, hysteria, bad skin, unsightly tics, ugly financial problems, maybe; but probably not peace of mind. I tell them that I think they ought to write anyway. But I try to make sure they understand that writing, and even getting good at it, and having books and stories and articles published, will not open the doors that most of them hope for. It will not make them well. It will not give them the feeling that the world has finally validated their parking tickets, that they have in fact finally arrived. My writer friends, and they are legion, do not go around beaming with quiet feelings of contentment. Most of them go around with haunted, abused, surprised looks on their faces, like lab dogs on whom very personal deodorant sprays have been tested.

My students do not want to hear this. Nor do they want to hear that it wasn't until my fourth book came out that I stopped being a starving artist. They do not want to hear that most of them probably won't get published and that even fewer will make enough to live on. But their fantasy of what it means to be published has very little to do with reality. So I tell them about my four-year-old son Sam, who goes to a little Christian preschool where he recently learned the story of Thanksgiving. A friend of his, who is also named Sam but who is twelve years old and very political, asked my Sam to tell him everything he knew about the holiday. So my Sam told him this lovely Christian-preschool version of Thanksgiving, with the pilgrims and the Native Americans and lots of lovely food and feelings. At which point Big Sam turned to me and said, somewhat bitterly, "I guess he hasn't heard about the small-pox-infected blankets yet."

Now, maybe we weren't handing out those blankets yet; maybe we were still on our good behavior. But the point is that my students, who so want to be published, have not yet heard about the small-pox-infected blankets of getting published. So that's one of the things I tell them.

But I also tell them that sometimes when my writer friends are working, they feel better and more alive than they do at any other time. And sometimes when they are writing well, they feel that they are living up to something. It is as if the right words, the true words, are already inside them, and they just want to help them get out. Writing this way is a little like milking a cow: the milk is so rich and delicious, and the cow is so glad you did it. I want the people who come to my classes to have this feeling, too.

So I tell them everything I've been thinking or talking about lately that has helped me get my work done. There are some quotes and examples from other writers that have inspired me and that I hand out every session. There are some things my friends remind me of when I call them, worried, bored, discouraged, and trying to scrounge together cab fare to the bridge. What follows in this book is what I've learned along the way, what I pass along to each new batch of students. This is not like other writing books, some of which are terrific. It's more personal, more like my classes. As of today, here is almost every single thing I know about writing.

Part One

Writing

Getting Started

The very first thing I tell my new students on the first day of a workshop is that good writing is about telling the truth. We are a species that needs and wants to understand who we are. Sheep lice do not seem to share this longing, which is one reason they write so very little. But we do. We have so much we want to say and figure out. Year after year my students are bursting with stories to tell, and they start writing projects with excitement and maybe even joy—finally their voices will be heard, and they are going to get to devote themselves to this one thing they've longed to do since childhood. But after a few days at the desk, telling the truth in an interesting way turns out to be about as easy and pleasurable as bathing a cat. Some lose faith. Their sense of self and story shatters and crumbles to the ground. Historically they show up for the first day of the workshop looking like bright goofy ducklings who will follow me anywhere, but by the time the second

3

class rolls around, they look at me as if the engagement is definitely off.

"I don't even know where to start," one will wail.

Start with your childhood, I tell them. Plug your nose and jump in, and write down all your memories as truthfully as you can. Flannery O'Connor said that anyone who survived childhood has enough material to write for the rest of his or her life. Maybe your childhood was grim and horrible, but grim and horrible is Okay if it is well done. Don't worry about doing it well yet, though. Just start getting it down.

Now, the amount of material may be so overwhelming that it can make your brain freeze. When I had been writing food reviews for a number of years, there were so many restaurants and individual dishes in my brainpan that when people asked for a recommendation, I couldn't think of a single restaurant where I'd ever actually eaten. But if the person could narrow it down to, say, Indian, I might remember one lavish Indian palace, where my date had asked the waiter for the Rudyard Kipling sampler and later for the holy-cow tartare. Then a number of memories would come to mind, of other dates and other Indian restaurants.

So you might start by writing down every single thing you can remember from your first few years in school. Start with kindergarten. Try to get the words and memories down as they occur to you. Don't worry if what you write is no good, because no one is going to see it. Move on to first grade, to second, to third. Who were your teachers, your classmates? What did you wear? Who and what were you jealous of? Now

4

branch out a little. Did your family take vacations during those years? Get these down on paper. Do you remember how much more presentable everybody else's family looked? Do you remember how when you'd be floating around in an inner tube on a river, your own family would have lost the little cap that screws over the airflow valve, so every time you got in and out of the inner tube, you'd scratch new welts in your thighs? And how other families never lost the caps?

If this doesn't pan out, or if it does but you finish mining this particular vein, see if focusing on holidays and big events helps you recollect your life as it was. Write down everything you can remember about every birthday or Christmas or Seder or Easter or whatever, every relative who was there. Write down all the stuff you swore you'd never tell another soul. What can you recall about your birthday parties—the disasters, the days of grace, your relatives' faces lit up by birthday candles? Scratch around for details: what people ate, listened to, wore—those terrible petaled swim caps, the men's awful trunks, the cocktail dress your voluptuous aunt wore that was so slinky she practically needed the Jaws of Life to get out of it. Write about the women's curlers with the bristles inside, the garters your father and uncles used to hold up their dress socks, your grandfathers' hats, your cousins' perfect Brownie uniforms, and how your own looked like it had just been hatched. Describe the trench coats and stoles and car coats, what they revealed and what they covered up. See if you can remember what you were given that Christmas when you were ten, and how it made you feel inside. Write down what the grown-ups said and did after they'd had a couple of dozen drinks, especially that one Fourth of July when your father made Fish House punch and the adults practically had to crawl from room to room.

Remember that you own what happened to you. If your childhood was less than ideal, you may have been raised thinking that if you told the truth about what really went on in your family, a long bony white finger would emerge from a cloud and point at you, while a chilling voice thundered, "We *told* you not to tell." But that was then. Just put down on paper everything you can remember now about your parents and siblings and relatives and neighbors, and we will deal with libel later on.

"But how?" my students ask. "How do you actually do it?"

You sit down, I say. You try to sit down at approximately the same time every day. This is how you train your unconscious to kick in for you creatively. So you sit down at, say, nine every morning, or ten every night. You put a piece of paper in the typewriter, or you turn on your computer and bring up the right file, and then you stare at it for an hour or so. You begin rocking, just a little at first, and then like a huge autistic child. You look at the ceiling, and over at the clock, yawn, and stare at the paper again. Then, with your fingers poised on the keyboard, you squint at an image that is forming in your mind—a scene, a locale, a character, whatever—and you try to quiet your mind so you can hear what that landscape or character has to say above the other voices in your mind. The other voices are banshees and drunken monkeys. They are the voices of anxiety, judgment, doom, guilt. Also, severe hypochondria. There may be a Nurse Ratched-like listing of things that must be done right this moment: foods that must come out of the freezer, appointments that must be canceled or made, hairs that must be tweezed. But you hold an imaginary gun to your head and make yourself stay at the desk. There is a vague pain at the base of your neck. It crosses your mind that you have meningitis. Then the phone rings and you look up at the ceiling with fury, summon every ounce of noblesse oblige, and answer the call politely, with maybe just the merest hint of irritation. The caller asks if you're working, and you say yeah, because you are.

Yet somehow in the face of all this, you clear a space for the writing voice, hacking away at the others with machetes, and you begin to compose sentences. You begin to string words together like beads to tell a story. You are desperate to communicate, to edify or entertain, to preserve moments of grace or joy or transcendence, to make real or imagined events come alive. But you cannot will this to happen. It is a matter of persistence and faith and hard work. So you might as well just go ahead and get started.

I wish I had a secret I could let you in on, some formula my father passed on to me in a whisper just before he died, some code word that has enabled me to sit at my desk and land flights of creative inspiration like an air-traffic controller. But I don't. All I know is that the process is pretty much the same for almost everyone I know. The good news is that some days it feels like you just have to keep getting out of your own way so that whatever it is that wants to be written can use you to write it. It is a little like when you have something difficult to discuss with someone, and as you go to do it, you hope and pray that the right words will come if only you show up and make a stab at it. And often the right words do come, and you—well—"write" for a while; you put a lot of thoughts down on paper. But the bad news is that if you're at all like me, you'll probably read over what you've written and spend the rest of the day obsessing, and praying that you do not die before you can completely rewrite or destroy what you have written, lest the eagerly waiting world learn how bad your first drafts are.

The obsessing may keep you awake, *or* the self-loathing may cause you to fall into a narcoleptic coma before dinner. But let's just say that you do fall asleep at a normal hour. Then the odds are that you will wake up at four in the morning, having dreamed that you have died. Death turns out to feel much more frantic than you had imagined. Typically you'll try to comfort yourself by thinking about the day's work—the day's excrementitious work. You may experience a jittery form of existential dread, considering the absolute meaninglessness of life and the fact that no one has ever really loved you; you may find yourself consumed with a free-floating shame, and a hopelessness about your work, and the realization that you will have to throw out everything you've done so far and start from scratch. But you will not be able to do so. Because you suddenly understand that you are completely riddled with cancer.

And then the miracle happens. The sun comes up again. So you get up and do your morning things, and one thing leads to another, and eventually, at nine, you find yourself back at the desk, staring blankly at the pages you filled yesterday. And there on page four is a paragraph with all sorts of life in it, smells and sounds and voices and colors and even a moment of dialogue that makes you say to yourself, very, very softly, "Hmmm." You look up and stare out the window again, but this time you are drumming your fingers on the desk, and you don't care about those first three pages; those you will throw out, those you needed to write to get to that fourth page, to get to that one long paragraph that was what you had in mind when you started, only you didn't know that, couldn't know that, until you got to it. And the story begins to materialize, and another thing is happening, which is that you are learning what you *aren't* writing, and this is helping you to find out what you *are* writing. Think of a fine painter attempting to capture an inner vision, beginning with one corner of the canvas, painting what he thinks should be there, not quite pulling it off, covering it over with white paint, and trying again, each time finding out what his painting isn't, until finally he finds out what it is.

And when you do find out what one corner of your vision is, you're off and running. And it really is like running. It always reminds me of the last lines of *Rabbit, Run*: "his heels hitting heavily on the pavement at first but with an effortless gathering out of a kind of sweet panic growing lighter and quicker and quieter, he runs. Ah: runs. Runs."

I wish I felt that kind of inspiration more often. I almost never do. All I know is that if I sit there long enough, something will happen.

My students stare at me for a moment. "How do we find an agent?" they ask.

I sigh. When you are ready, there are books that list agents. You can select a few names and write to them and ask if they would like to take a look at your work. Mostly they will not want to. But if you are really good, and very persistent, someone eventually will read your material and take you on. I can almost promise you this. However, in the meantime, we are going to concentrate on writing itself, on how to become a better writer, because, for one thing, becoming a better writer is going to help you become a better reader, and *that* is the real payoff.

But my students don't believe me. They want agents, and to be published. And they also want refunds.

Almost all of them have been writing at least for a little while, some of them all of their lives. Many of them have been told over the years that they are quite good, and they want to know why they feel so crazy when they sit down to work, why they have these wonderful ideas and then they sit down and write one sentence and see with horror that it is a bad one, and then every major form of mental illness from which they suffer surfaces, leaping out of the water like trout—the delusions, hypochondria, the grandiosity, the self-loathing, the inability to track one thought to completion, even the hand-washing fixation, the Howard Hughes germ phobias. And especially, the paranoia.

You can be defeated and disoriented by all these feelings, I tell them, or you can see the paranoia, for instance, as wonderful material. You can use it as the raw clay that you pull out of the river: surely one of your characters is riddled with it, and so in giving that person this particular quality, you get to use it, shape it into something true and funny or frightening. I read them a poem by Phillip Lopate that someone once sent me, that goes:

> *We who are*
> *your closest friends*
> *feel the time*
> *has come to tell you*
> *that every Thursday*
> *we have been meeting,*
> *as a group,*
> *to devise ways*
> *to keep you*
> *in perpetual uncertainty*
> *frustration*
> *discontent and*
> *torture*
> *by neither loving you*
> *as much as you want*
> *nor cutting you adrift.*

11

Your analyst is
in on it,
plus your boyfriend
and your ex-husband;
and we have pledged
to disappoint you
as long as you need us.
In announcing our
association
we realize we have
placed in your hands
a possible antidote
against uncertainty
indeed against ourselves.
But since our Thursday nights
have brought us
to a community
of purpose
rare in itself
with you as
the natural center,
we feel hopeful you
will continue to make unreasonable
demands for affection
if not as a consequence
of your disastrous personality
then for the good of the collective.

They stare at me like the cast of *One Flew Over the Cuckoo Nest*. Only about three of them think this poem is funny, or even a good example of someone taking his own paranoia and shaping it into something artistic and true. A few people look haunted. The ones who most want to be published just think I'm an extremely angry person. Some of them look emotionally broken, some look at me with actual disgust, as if I am standing there naked under fluorescent lights.

Finally someone will raise his or her hand. "Can you send your manuscript directly to a publisher, or do you really need an agent?"

After a moment or so, I say, You really need an agent.

The problem that comes up over and over again is that these people want to be published. They *kind* of want to write, but they *really* want to be published. You'll never get to where you want to be that way, I tell them. There is a door we all want to walk through, and writing can help you find it and open it. Writing can give you what having a baby can give you: it can get you to start paying attention, can help you soften, can wake you up. But publishing won't do any of those things; you'll never get in that way.

My son, Sam, at three and a half, had these keys to a set of plastic handcuffs, and one morning he intentionally locked himself out of the house. I was sitting on the couch reading the newspaper when I heard him stick his plastic keys into the doorknob and try to open the door. Then I heard him say, "Oh, shit." My whole face widened, like the guy in Edvard

Munch's *Scream*. After a moment I got up and opened the front door.

"Honey," I said, "what'd you just say?"

"I said, 'Oh, shit,' " he said.

"But, honey, that's a naughty word. *Both* of us have absolutely got to stop using it. Okay?"

He hung his head for a moment, nodded, and said, "Okay, Mom." Then he leaned forward and said confidentially, "But I'll tell you why I said 'shit.' " I said Okay, and he said, "Because of the fucking keys!"

Fantasy keys won't get you in. Almost every single thing you hope publication will do for you is a fantasy, a hologram— it's the eagle on your credit card that only seems to soar. What's real is that if you do your scales every day, if you slowly try harder and harder pieces, if you listen to great musicians play music you love, you'll get better. At times when you're working, you'll sit there feeling hung over and bored, and you may or may not be able to pull yourself up out of it that day. But it is fantasy to think that successful writers do not have these bored, defeated hours, these hours of deep insecurity when one feels as small and jumpy as a water bug. They do. But they also often feel a great sense of amazement that they get to write, and they know that this is what they want to do for the rest of their lives. And so if one of your heart's deepest longings is to *write,* there are ways to get your work done, and a number of reasons why it is important to do so.

And what are those reasons again? my students ask.

Because for some of us, books are as important as almost anything else on earth. What a miracle it is that out of these small, flat, rigid squares of paper unfolds world after world after world, worlds that sing to you, comfort and quiet or excite you. Books help us understand who we are and how we are to behave. They show us what community and friendship mean; they show us how to live and die. They are full of all the things that you don't get in real life—wonderful, lyrical language, for instance, right off the bat. And quality of attention: we may notice amazing details during the course of a day but we rarely let ourselves stop and really pay attention. An author *makes* you notice, makes you pay attention, and this is a great gift. My gratitude for good writing is unbounded; I'm grateful for it the way I'm grateful for the ocean. Aren't you? I ask.

Most of them nod. This is why they are here: they love to read, they love good writing, they want to do it, too. But a few of the students are still looking at me with a sense of betrayal or hopelessness, as if they are thinking of hanging themselves. Too late for a refund, I tell them cheerfully, but I have something even better. Next are the two single most helpful things I can tell you about writing.

S h o r t   A s s i g n m e n t s

The first useful concept is the idea of short assignments. Often when you sit down to write, what you have in mind is an autobiographical novel about your childhood, or a play about the immigrant experience, or a history of—oh, say—say women. But this is like trying to scale a glacier. It's hard to get your footing, and your fingertips get all red and frozen and torn up. Then your mental illnesses arrive at the desk like your sickest, most secretive relatives. And they pull up chairs in a semicircle around the computer, and they try to be quiet but you know they are there with their weird coppery breath, leering at you behind your back.

What I do at this point, as the panic mounts and the jungle drums begin beating and I realize that the well has run dry and that my future is behind me and I'm going to have to get a job only I'm completely unemployable, is to stop. First I try to breathe, because I'm either sitting there panting like a lapdog or I'm unintentionally making slow asthmatic death rattles. So I just sit there for a minute, breathing slowly, quietly. I let my mind wander. After a moment I may notice that I'm trying to decide whether or not I am too old for orthodontia and whether right now would be a good time to make a few calls, and then I start to think about learning to use makeup and how maybe I could find some boyfriend who is not a total and complete fixer-upper and then my life would be totally great and I'd be happy all the time, and then I think about all the people I should have called back before I sat down to work, and how I should probably at least check in with my agent and tell him this great idea I have and see if he thinks it's a good idea, and see if *he* thinks I need orthodontia—if that is what he is actually thinking whenever we have lunch together. Then I think about someone I'm really annoyed with, or some financial problem that is driving me crazy, and decide that I must resolve this before I get down to today's work. So I become a dog with a chew toy, worrying it for a while, wrestling it to the ground, flinging it over my shoulder, chasing it, licking it, chewing it, flinging it back over my shoulder. I stop just short of actually barking. But all of this only takes somewhere between one and two minutes, so I haven't actually wasted that much time. Still, it leaves me winded. I go back to trying to breathe, slowly and calmly, and I finally notice the one-inch picture frame that I put on my desk to remind me of short assignments.

It reminds me that all I have to do is to write down as much as I can see through a one-inch picture frame. This is all I have to bite off for the time being. All I am going to do right now, for example, is write that one paragraph that sets the story in my hometown, in the late fifties, when the trains were still running. I am going to paint a picture of it, in words, on my word processor. Or all I am going to do is to describe the main character the very first time we meet her, when she first walks out the front door and onto the porch. I am not even going to describe the expression on her face when she first notices the blind dog sitting behind the wheel of her car—just what I can see through the one-inch picture frame, just one paragraph describing this woman, in the town where I grew up, the first time we encounter her.

E. L. Doctorow once said that "writing a novel is like driving a car at night. You can see only as far as your headlights, but you can make the whole trip that way." You don't have to see where you're going, you don't have to see your destination or everything you will pass along the way. You just have to see two or three feet ahead of you. This is right up there with the best advice about writing, or life, I have ever heard.

So after I've completely exhausted myself thinking about the people I most resent in the world, and my more arresting financial problems, and, of course, the orthodontia, I remember to pick up the one-inch picture frame and to figure out a one-inch piece of my story to tell, one small scene, one memory, one exchange. I also remember a story that I know I've told elsewhere but that over and over helps me to get a grip: thirty years ago my older brother, who was ten years old at the time, was trying to get a report on birds written that he'd had three months to write, which was due the next day. We were out at our family cabin in Bolinas, and he was at the kitchen table close to tears, surrounded by binder paper and pencils and unopened books on birds, immobilized by the hugeness of the task ahead. Then my father sat down beside him, put his arm around my brother's shoulder, and said, "Bird by bird, buddy. Just take it bird by bird."

I tell this story again because it usually makes a dent in the tremendous sense of being overwhelmed that my students experience. Sometimes it actually gives them hope, and hope, as Chesterton said, is the power of being cheerful in circumstances that we know to be desperate. Writing can be a pretty desperate endeavor, because it is about some of our deepest needs: our need to be visible, to be heard, our need to make sense of our lives, to wake up and grow and belong. It is no wonder if we sometimes tend to take ourselves perhaps a bit too seriously. So here is another story I tell often.

In the Bill Murray movie *Stripes,* in which he joins the army, there is a scene that takes place the first night of boot camp, where Murray's platoon is assembled in the barracks. They are supposed to be getting to know their sergeant, played by Warren Oates, and one another. So each man takes a few moments to say a few things about who he is and where he is from. Finally it is the turn of this incredibly intense, angry guy named Francis. "My name is Francis," he says. "No one calls me Francis—anyone here calls me Francis and I'll kill them. And another thing. I don't like to be touched. Anyone here ever tries to touch me, I'll kill them," at which point Warren Oates jumps in and says, "Hey—lighten up, Francis."

This is not a bad line to have taped to the wall of your office.

Say to yourself in the kindest possible way, Look, honey, all we're going to do for now is to write a description of the river at sunrise, or the young child swimming in the pool at the club, or the first time the man sees the woman he will marry. That is all we are going to do for now. We are just going to take this bird by bird. But we are going to finish this *one* short assignment.

Shitty First Drafts

Now, practically even better news than that of short assignments is the idea of shitty first drafts. All good writers write them. This is how they end up with good second drafts and terrific third drafts. People tend to look at successful writers, writers who are getting their books published and maybe even doing well financially, and think that they sit down at their desks every morning feeling like a million dollars, feeling great about who they are and how much talent they have and what a great story they have to tell; that they take in a few deep breaths, push back their sleeves, roll their necks a few times to get all the cricks out, and dive in, typing fully formed passages as fast as a court reporter. But this is just the fantasy of the uninitiated. I know some very great writers, writers you love who write beautifully and have made a great deal of money, and not *one* of them sits down routinely feeling wildly enthusiastic and confident. Not one of them writes elegant first drafts. All right, one of them does, but we do not like her very much. We do not think that she has a rich inner life or that God likes her or can even stand her. (Although when I mentioned this to my priest friend Tom, he said you can safely assume you've created God in your own image when it turns out that God hates all the same people you do.)

Very few writers really know what they are doing until they've done it. Nor do they go about their business feeling dewy and thrilled. They do not type a few stiff warm-up sentences and then find themselves bounding along like huskies across the snow. One writer I know tells me that he sits down every morning and says to himself nicely, "It's not like you don't have a choice, because you do—you can either type or kill yourself." We all often feel like we are pulling teeth, even those writers whose prose ends up being the most natural and fluid. The right words and sentences just do not come pouring out like ticker tape most of the time. Now, Muriel Spark is said to have felt that she was taking dictation from God every morning—sitting there, one supposes, plugged into a Dicta-phone, typing away, humming. But this is a very hostile and aggressive position. One might hope for bad things to rain down on a person like this.

For me and most of the other writers I know, writing is not rapturous. In fact, the only way I can get anything written at all is to write really, really shitty first drafts.

The first draft is the child's draft, where you let it all pour out and then let it romp all over the place, knowing that no one is going to see it and that you can shape it later. You just let this childlike part of you channel whatever voices and visions come through and onto the page. If one of the characters wants to say, "Well, so what, Mr. Poopy Pants?," you let her. No one is going to see it. If the kid wants to get into really sentimental, weepy, emotional territory, you let him. Just get it all down on paper, because there may be something great in those six crazy pages that you would never have gotten to by more rational, grown-up means. There may be something in the very last line of the very last paragraph on page six that you just love, that is so beautiful or wild that you now know what you're supposed to be writing about, more or less, or in what direction you might go—but there was no way to get to this without first getting through the first five and a half pages.

I used to write food reviews for *California* magazine before it folded. (My writing food reviews had nothing to do with the magazine folding, although every single review did cause a couple of canceled subscriptions. Some readers took umbrage at my comparing mounds of vegetable puree with various ex-presidents' brains.) These reviews always took two days to write. First I'd go to a restaurant several times with a few opinionated, articulate friends in tow. I'd sit there writing down everything anyone said that was at all interesting or funny. Then on the following Monday I'd sit down at my desk with my notes, and try to write the review. Even after I'd been doing this for years, panic would set in. I'd try to write a lead, but instead I'd write a couple of dreadful sentences,

XX them out, try again, XX everything out, and then feel despair
and worry settle on my chest like an x-ray apron. It's over,
I'd think, calmly. I'm not going to be able to get the magic
to work this time. I'm ruined. I'm through. I'm toast. Maybe,
I'd think, I can get my old job back as a clerk-typist. But
probably not. I'd get up and study my teeth in the mirror for
a while. Then I'd stop, remember to breathe, make a few
phone calls, hit the kitchen and chow down. Eventually I'd
go back and sit down at my desk, and sigh for the next ten
minutes. Finally I would pick up my one-inch picture frame,
stare into it as if for the answer, and every time the answer
would come: all I had to do was to write a really shitty first
draft of, say, the opening paragraph. And no one was going
to see it.

So I'd start writing without reining myself in. It was almost
just typing, just making my fingers move. And the writing
would be *terrible*. I'd write a lead paragraph that was a whole
page, even though the entire review could only be three pages
long, and then I'd start writing up descriptions of the food,
one dish at a time, bird by bird, and the critics would be
sitting on my shoulders, commenting like cartoon characters.
They'd be pretending to snore, or rolling their eyes at my
overwrought descriptions, no matter how hard I tried to tone
those descriptions down, no matter how conscious I was of
what a friend said to me gently in my early days of restaurant
reviewing. "Annie," she said, "it is just a piece of *chick*en. It
is just a bit of *cake*."

But because by then I had been writing for so long, I would

eventually let myself trust the process—sort of, more or less. I'd write a first draft that was maybe twice as long as it should be, with a self-indulgent and boring beginning, stupefying descriptions of the meal, lots of quotes from my black-humored friends that made them sound more like the Manson girls than food lovers, and no ending to speak of. The whole thing would be so long and incoherent and hideous that for the rest of the day I'd obsess about getting creamed by a car before I could write a decent second draft. I'd worry that people would read what I'd written and believe that the accident had really been a suicide, that I had panicked because my talent was waning and my mind was shot.

The next day, though, I'd sit down, go through it all with a colored pen, take out everything I possibly could, find a new lead somewhere on the second page, figure out a kicky place to end it, and then write a second draft. It always turned out fine, sometimes even funny and weird and helpful. I'd go over it one more time and mail it in.

Then, a month later, when it was time for another review, the whole process would start again, complete with the fears that people would find my first draft before I could rewrite it.

Almost all good writing begins with terrible first efforts. You need to start somewhere. Start by getting something—anything—down on paper. A friend of mine says that the first draft is the down draft—you just get it down. The second draft is the up draft—you fix it up. You try to say what you have to say more accurately. And the third draft is the dental draft, where you check every tooth, to see if it's loose or cramped or decayed, or even, God help us, healthy.

What I've learned to do when I sit down to work on a shitty first draft is to quiet the voices in my head. First there's the vinegar-lipped Reader Lady, who says primly, "Well, *that's* not very interesting, is it?" And there's the emaciated German male who writes these Orwellian memos detailing your thought crimes. And there are your parents, agonizing over your lack of loyalty and discretion; and there's William Burroughs, dozing off or shooting up because he finds you as bold and articulate as a houseplant; and so on. And there are also the dogs: let's not forget the dogs, the dogs in their pen who will surely hurtle and snarl their way out if you ever *stop* writing, because writing is, for some of us, the latch that keeps the door of the pen closed, keeps those crazy ravenous dogs contained.

Quieting these voices is at least half the battle I fight daily. But this is better than it used to be. It used to be 87 percent. Left to its own devices, my mind spends much of its time having conversations with people who aren't there. I walk along defending myself to people, or exchanging repartee with them, or rationalizing my behavior, or seducing them with gossip, or pretending I'm on their TV talk show or whatever. I speed or run an aging yellow light or don't come to a full stop, and one nanosecond later am explaining to imaginary cops exactly why I had to do what I did, or insisting that I did not in fact do it.

I happened to mention this to a hypnotist I saw many years

ago, and he looked at me very nicely. At first I thought he was feeling around on the floor for the silent alarm button, but then he gave me the following exercise, which I still use to this day.

Close your eyes and get quiet for a minute, until the chatter starts up. Then isolate one of the voices and imagine the person speaking as a mouse. Pick it up by the tail and drop it into a mason jar. Then isolate another voice, pick it up by the tail, drop it in the jar. And so on. Drop in any high-maintenance parental units, drop in any contractors, lawyers, colleagues, children, anyone who is whining in your head. Then put the lid on, and watch all these mouse people clawing at the glass, jabbering away, trying to make you feel like shit because you won't do what they want—won't give them more money, won't be more successful, won't see them more often. Then imagine that there is a volume-control button on the bottle. Turn it all the way up for a minute, and listen to the stream of angry, neglected, guilt-mongering voices. Then turn it all the way down and watch the frantic mice lunge at the glass, trying to get to you. Leave it down, and get back to your shitty first draft.

A writer friend of mine suggests opening the jar and shooting them all in the head. But I think he's a little angry, and I'm sure nothing like this would ever occur to you.

Perfectionism

Perfectionism is the voice of the oppressor, the enemy of the people. It will keep you cramped and insane your whole life, and it is the main obstacle between you and a shitty first draft. I think perfectionism is based on the obsessive belief that if you run carefully enough, hitting each stepping-stone just right, you won't have to die. The truth is that you will die anyway and that a lot of people who aren't even looking at their feet are going to do a whole lot better than you, and have a lot more fun while they're doing it.

Besides, perfectionism will ruin your writing, blocking inventiveness and playfulness and life force (these are words we are allowed to use in California). Perfectionism means that you try desperately not to leave so much mess to clean up. But clutter and mess show us that life is being lived. Clutter is wonderfully fertile ground—you can still discover new treasures under all those piles, clean things up, edit things out, fix things, get a grip. Tidiness suggests that something is as good as it's going to get. Tidiness makes me think of held breath, of suspended animation, while writing needs to breathe and move.

When I was twenty-one, I had my tonsils removed. I was one of those people who got strep throat every few minutes, and my doctor finally decided that I needed to have my tonsils taken out. For the entire week afterward, swallowing hurt so much that I could barely open my mouth for a straw. I had a prescription for painkillers, though, and when they ran out but the pain hadn't, I called the nurse and said that she would really need to send another prescription over, and maybe a little mixed grill of drugs because I was also feeling somewhat anxious. But she wouldn't. I asked to speak to her supervisor. She told me her supervisor was at lunch and that I needed to buy some *gum,* of all things, and to chew it vigorously—the thought of which made me clutch at my throat. She explained that when we have a wound in our body, the nearby muscles cramp around it to protect it from any more violation and from infection, and that I would need to use these muscles if I wanted them to relax again. So finally my best friend Pammy went out and bought me some gum, and I began to chew it, with great hostility and skepticism. The first bites caused a ripping sensation in the back of my throat, but within minutes all the pain was gone, permanently.

I think that something similar happens with our psychic muscles. They cramp around our wounds—the pain from our childhood, the losses and disappointments of adulthood, the humiliations suffered in both——to keep us from getting hurt in the same place again, to keep foreign substances out. So those wounds never have a chance to heal. Perfectionism is one way our muscles cramp. In some cases we don't even know that the wounds and the cramping are there, but both limit us. They keep us moving and writing in tight, worried ways. They keep us standing back or backing away from life, keep us from experiencing life in a naked and immediate way. So how do we break through them and get on?

It's easier if you believe in God, but not impossible if you don't. If you believe, then this God of yours might be capable of relieving you of some of this perfectionism. Still, one of the most annoying things about God is that he never just touches you with his magic wand, like Glinda the Good, and gives you what you want. Like it would be so much skin off his nose. But he might give you the courage or the stamina to write lots and lots of terrible first drafts, and then you'd learn that good second drafts can spring from these, and you'd see that big sloppy imperfect messes have value.

Now, it might be that your God is an uptight, judgmental perfectionist, sort of like Bob Dole or, for that matter, me. But a priest friend of mine has cautioned me away from the standard God of our childhoods, who loves and guides you and then, if you are bad, roasts you: God as high school principal in a gray suit who never remembered your name but is always leafing unhappily through your files. If this is your God, maybe you need to blend in the influence of someone who is ever so slightly more amused by you, someone less anal. David Byrne is good, for instance. Gracie Allen is good. Mr. Rogers will work.

If you don't believe in God, it may help to remember this great line of Geneen Roth's: that awareness is learning to keep yourself company. And then learn to be more *compassionate* company, as if you were somebody you are fond of and wish to encourage. I doubt that you would read a close friend's early efforts and, in his or her presence, roll your eyes and snicker. I doubt that you would pantomime sticking your finger down your throat. I think you might say something along the lines of, "Good for you. We can work out some of the problems later, but for now, full steam ahead!"

In any case, the bottom line is that if you want to write, you get to, but you probably won't be able to get very far if you don't start trying to get over your perfectionism. You set out to tell a story of some sort, to tell the truth as you feel it, because something is calling you to do so. It calls you like the beckoning finger of smoke in cartoons that rises off the pie cooling on the windowsill, slides under doors and into mouse holes or into the nostrils of the sleeping man or woman in the easy chair. Then the aromatic smoke crooks its finger, and the mouse or the man or woman rises and follows, nose in the air. But some days the smoke is faint and you just have to follow it as best you can, sniffing away. Still, even on those days, you might notice how great perseverance feels. And the next day the scent may seem stronger—or it may just be that you are developing a quiet doggedness. This is priceless. Perfectionism, on the other hand, will only drive you mad.

Your day's work might turn out to have been a mess. So what? Vonnegut said, "When I write, I feel like an armless legless man with a crayon in his mouth." So go ahead and make big scrawls and mistakes. Use up lots of paper. Perfectionism is a mean, frozen form of idealism, while messes are the artist's true friend. What people somehow (inadvertently, I'm sure) forgot to mention when we were children was that we need to make messes in order to find out who we are and why we are here——and, by extension, what we're supposed to be writing.

School Lunches

I know I set out to tell you every single thing I know about writing, but I am also going to tell you every single thing I know about school lunches, partly because the longings and dynamics and anxieties are so similar. I think this will also show how taking short assignments and then producing really shitty first drafts of these assignments can yield a bounty of detailed memory, raw material, and strange characters lurking in the shadows. So: sometimes when a student calls and is mewling and puking about the hopelessness of trying to put words down on paper, I ask him or her to tell me about school lunches—at parochial schools, private schools, twenty years earlier than mine, or ten years later, in Southern California or New York. And they always turn out to be similar to my middle-class Northern California public school lunches. But in important ways they are different, too, and this is even more interesting, for the obvious reason that when we study the differences, we see in bolder relief what we have in common. And for some strange reason, when my students start to jam with me about school lunches, they get off the phone feeling more enthusiastic and in better shape.

One time, in one of my classes, I asked my students to write about lunches for half an hour, and I sat down with them and wrote:

Here is the main thing I know about public school lunches: it only looked like a bunch of kids eating lunch. It was really about opening our insides in front of everyone. Just like writing is. It was a precursor of the showers in seventh- and eighth-grade gym, where everyone could see your everything or your lack of everything, and smell the inside smells of your body, and the whole time you just knew you were going to catch something. The contents of your lunch said whether or not you and your family were Okay. Some bag lunches, like some people, were Okay, and some weren't. There was a code, a right and acceptable way. It was that simple.

But in half an hour there was already too much material for me and some of the people in class, and it threatened to immobilize us. So we decided not even to bother with our parents' handwriting on the outside of the brown paper lunch bag—how much it resembled a Turkish assassin's and what that said about us. We decided to set aside the bag itself for a moment. For the time being we'd stick with the contents, and, to begin with, the sandwich. That was the one-inch picture frame we were going to look through.

Your sandwich was the centerpiece, and there were strict guidelines. It almost goes without saying that store-bought white bread was the only acceptable bread. There were no exceptions. If your mother made the white bread for your sandwich, you could only hope that no one would notice. You certainly did not brag about it, any more than you would brag that she also made headcheese. And there were only a few things that your parents could put in between the two pieces of bread. Bologna was fine, salami and unaggressive cheese were fine, peanut butter and jelly were fine if your parents understood the jelly/jam issue.

Grape jelly was best, by far, a nice slippery comforting sugary petroleum-product grape. Strawberry jam was second; everything else was iffy. Take raspberry, for instance—

Now, see, I couldn't remember, as I wrote in class, just exactly what it was about raspberry jam that was so disconcerting. So when I got home that night, I called a friend who is also a writer, very successful and maybe the most neurotic person I know. I said, Remember how in elementary school, grape jelly was best in your lunch, strawberry jam was Okay, but raspberry was real borderline? Can you talk to me about your experiences with these things? And my friend went into an impassioned, disoriented riff about how there was too much happening in raspberry jam, too many seeds per spoonful. It felt like there were all these tiny little pod people in it. It was *Body-Snatcher* jam.

My friend then mentioned apricot jam, which was even worse than raspberry. I had not thought about this in thirty

35

years, but now it all came back with horrible clarity. Apricot jam looked too much like glue, or mucilage. But you could count on having apricot jam when your father made the lunch. Fathers loved apricot jam; I don't know why, but I'm sure Anna Freud could have a field day with it.

I sat down that night and kept writing:

In general, come to think of it, when fathers made lunches, things always turned out badly. Fathers were so oblivious back then. They were like foreigners. For instance, a code bologna sandwich meant white bread, one or two slices of bologna, mustard, one wilted piece of iceberg lettuce. (The Catholics were heavily into mayonnaise, which we might get into later.) Fathers, to begin with, always used nonregulation bread and then buttered it, which made the sandwich about as tradable as a plate of haggis. Also, everything was always falling out of the sandwiches fathers made. I'm not sure why. They'd use anything green and frilly for lettuce, when of course only the one piece of wilted iceberg was permissible. Your friends saw a big leaf of romaine falling out along with the slice of bologna, and you might soon find yourself alongside the kid against the fence.

There was always that one kid against the fence. How could the rest of us feel Okay if there wasn't? If it was a guy, there was probably a trumpet case at his feet and he wore strangely scuffed shoes, because he avoided the foot traffic on sidewalks and walked instead through weedy lots with dogs yipping at him. He didn't end up at that station only because his lunches were nightmarish in their eccentricity, but his lunches didn't help.

He almost certainly ended up being a writer.

Now, who knows if any of this is usable material? There's no way to tell until you've got it all down, and then there might just be one sentence or one character or one theme that you end up using. But you get it all down. You just *write*.

I heard Natalie Goldberg, the author of *Writing Down the Bones,* speak on writing once. Someone asked her for the best possible writing advice she had to offer, and she held up a yellow legal pad, pretended her fingers held a pen, and scribbled away. I think this was some sort of Zen reference—the Buddhist disciple remembering Buddha's flower sermon, in which all Buddha did was hold up a flower and twirl it, in silence, sitting on the mountain. Me, I'm a nice Christian girl, and while I wish I could quote something kicky and inspirational that Jesus had to say about writing, the truth is that when students ask me for the best practical advice I know, I always pick up a piece of paper and pantomime scribbling away. My students usually think this is a very wise and Zenlike thing for me to convey. Mostly, I forget to give Natalie Goldberg credit.

But write about what? they ask next.

Write about carrot sticks, I tell them:

Code carrots had to look machine extruded, absolutely uniform, none longer than the length of the sandwich. Your parents would sometimes send you to school with waxed-paper packets of uneven cuckoo-bunny carrots, and your carrot esteem would be so low you couldn't even risk looking at the guy against the fence. Bad juju. If you so much as glanced at him, a visible empathetic arc would stretch between you, almost like a rainbow, and link you two in the minds of your peers forever.

And then there was the matter of the wrapping paper; waxed paper and later Saran wrap. If code lunches were about that intense desire for one thing in life to be Okay, or even just to appear to be Okay, when all around you and at home and inside you things were so chaotic and painful, then it mattered that it not look like Jughead had wrapped your sandwich. A code lunch suggested that someone in your family was paying attention, even if in your heart you knew that your parents were screwing up left and right. So it was a little like making your bed at lunch. Everything should be squared. Sandwiches should be wrapped with hospital corners. Right?

Okay. That's all. But now I have this material to choose from, to work with, to shape, edit, highlight, or toss. (And that's very nice of you to suggest the latter.) This is my version of school lunches. Yours might be different and I would be interested in hearing about it. (Now don't get me wrong. I am not suggesting you mail it to me. But I bet it reveals some interesting stuff about you and your family and the times in which you grew up.) And even though what I've quoted here is shitty-first-draft stuff, the boy against the fence appeared out of nowhere—I had no idea when I started writing that he was in my memory. To me, he is the most important thing that came out of this exercise. Tomorrow when I sit down to work on my novel, he will be someone who matters to me, whom I want to work with, get to know, who has something important to say or somewhere only he can take me.

Polaroids

Writing a first draft is very much like watching a Polaroid develop. You can't—and, in fact, you're not supposed to— know exactly what the picture is going to look like until it has finished developing. First you just point at what has your attention and take the picture. In the last chapter, for instance, what had my attention were the contents of my lunch bag. But as the picture developed, I found I had a really clear image of the boy against the fence. Or maybe *your* Polaroid was supposed to be a picture of that boy against the fence, and you didn't notice until the last minute that a family was standing a few feet away from him. Now, maybe it's his family, or the family of one of the kids in his class, but at any rate these people are going to be in the photograph, too. Then the film emerges from the camera with a grayish green murkiness that gradually becomes clearer and clearer, and finally you see the husband and wife holding their baby with two children standing beside them. And at first it all seems very sweet, but then the shadows begin to appear, and then you start to see the animal tragedy, the baboons baring their teeth. And then you see a flash of bright red flowers in the bottom left quadrant that you didn't even know were in the picture when you took it, and these flowers evoke a time or a memory that moves you mysteriously. And finally, as the portrait comes into focus, you begin to notice all the props surrounding these people, and you begin to understand how props define us and comfort us, and show us what we value and what we need, and who we think we are.

You couldn't have had any way of knowing what this piece of work would look like when you first started. You just knew that there was something about these people that compelled you, and you stayed with that something long enough for it to show you what it was about.

Watch this Polaroid develop:

Six or seven years ago I was asked to write an article on the Special Olympics. I had been going to the local event for years, partly because a couple of friends of mine compete. Also, I love sports, and I love to watch athletes, special or otherwise. So I showed up this time with a great deal of interest but no real sense of what the finished article might look like.

Things tend to go very, very slowly at the Special Olympics. It is not like trying to cover the Preakness. Still, it has its own exhilaration, and I cheered and took notes all morning.

The last track-and-field event before lunch was a twenty-five-yard race run by some unusually handicapped runners and walkers, many of whom seemed completely confused. They lumped and careened along, one man making a snail-slow break for the stands, one heading out toward the steps where the winners receive their medals; both of them were shepherded back. The race took just about forever. And here it was nearly noon and we were all so hungry. Finally, though, everyone crossed over the line, and those of us in the stands got up to go—when we noticed that way down the track, four or five yards from the starting line, was another runner.

She was a girl of about sixteen with a normal-looking face above a wracked and emaciated body. She was on metal crutches, and she was just plugging along, one tiny step after another, moving one crutch forward two or three inches, then moving a leg, then moving the other crutch two or three inches, then moving the other leg. It was just excruciating. Plus, I was starving to death. Inside I was going, Come on, come on, come on, swabbing at my forehead with anxiety, while she kept taking these two- or three-inch steps forward. What felt like four hours later, she crossed the finish line, and you could see that she was absolutely stoked, in a shy, girlish way.

A tall African American man with no front teeth fell into step with me as I left the bleachers to go look for some lunch. He tugged on the sleeve of my sweater, and I looked up at him, and he handed me a Polaroid someone had taken of him and his friends that day. "Look at us," he said. His speech was difficult to understand, thick and slow as a warped record.

41

His two friends in the picture had Down's syndrome. All three of them looked extremely pleased with themselves. I admired the picture and then handed it back to him. He stopped, so I stopped, too. He pointed to his own image. "That," he said, "is one cool man."

And this was the image from which an article began forming, although I could not have told you exactly what the piece would end up being about. I just knew that something had started to emerge.

After lunch I wandered over to the auditorium, where it turned out a men's basketball game was in progress. The African American man with no front teeth was the star of the game. You could tell that he was because even though no one had made a basket yet, his teammates almost always passed him the ball. Even the people on the *other* team passed him the ball a lot. In lieu of any scoring, the men stampeded in slow motion up and down the court, dribbling the ball thunderously. I had never heard such a loud game. It was all sort of crazily beautiful. I imagined describing the game for my article and then for my students: the loudness, the joy. I kept replaying the scene of the girl on crutches making her way up the track to the finish line—and all of a sudden my article began to appear out of the grayish green murk. And I could see that it was about tragedy transformed over the years into joy. It was about the beauty of sheer effort. I could see it almost as clearly as I could the photograph of that one cool man and his two friends.

The auditorium bleachers were packed. Then a few minutes

later, still with no score on the board, the tall black man dribbled slowly from one end of the court to the other, and heaved the ball up into the air, and it dropped into the basket. The crowd roared, and all the men on both teams looked up wide-eyed at the hoop, as if it had just burst into flames.

You would have loved it, I tell my students. You would have felt like you could write all day.

Character

Knowledge of your characters also emerges the way a Polaroid develops: it takes time for you to know them. One image that helps me begin to know the people in my fiction is something a friend once told me. She said that every single one of us at birth is given an emotional acre all our own. You get one, your awful Uncle Phil gets one, I get one, Tricia Nixon gets one, everyone gets one. And as long as you don't hurt anyone, you really get to do with your acre as you please. You can plant fruit trees or flowers or alphabetized rows of vegetables, or nothing at all. If you want your acre to look like a giant garage sale, or an auto-wrecking yard, that's what you get to do with it. There's a fence around your acre, though, with a gate, and if people keep coming onto your land and sliming it or trying to get you to do what they think is right, you get to ask them to leave. And they have to go, because this is your acre.

By the same token, each of your characters has an emotional acre that they tend, or don't tend, in certain specific ways. One of the things you want to discover as you start out is what each person's acre looks like. What is the person growing, and what sort of shape is the land in? This knowledge may not show up per se in what you write, but the point is that you need to find out as much as possible about the interior life of the people you are working with.

Now, you also want to ask yourself how they stand, what they carry in their pockets or purses, what happens in their faces and to their posture when they are thinking, or bored, or afraid. Whom would they have voted for last time? Why should we care about them anyway? What would be the first thing they stopped doing if they found out they had six months to live? Would they start smoking again? Would they keep flossing?

You are going to love some of your characters, because they are you or some facet of you, and you are going to hate some of your characters for the same reason. But no matter what, you are probably going to have to let bad things happen to some of the characters you love or you won't have much of a story. Bad things happen to good characters, because our actions have consequences, and we do not all behave perfectly all the time. As soon as you start protecting your characters from the ramifications of their less-than-lofty behavior, your story will start to feel flat and pointless, just like in real life. Get to know your characters as well as you can, let there be something at stake, and then let the chips fall where they may.

My Al-Anon friend told me about the frazzled, defeated wife of an alcoholic man who kept passing out on the front lawn in the middle of the night. The wife kept dragging him in before dawn so that the neighbors wouldn't see him, until finally an old black woman from the South came up to her one day after a meeting and said, "Honey? Leave him lay where Jesus flang him." And I am slowly, slowly in my work—and even more slowly in real life—learning to do this.

A man I know once said to me, "The evidence is in, and you are the verdict." This will be true for each of your characters. The evidence will be in, and each of them will be his or her own verdict. But you may not know what this verdict is at first. You may only know your characters' externals instead of their essences. Don't worry about it. More will be revealed over time. In the meantime, can you see what your people look like? What sort of first impression do they make? What does each one care most about, want more than anything in the world? What are their secrets? How do they move, how do they smell? Everyone is walking around as an advertisement for who he or she is—so who is this person? Show us. What-ever your characters do or say will be born out of who they are, so you need to set out to get to know each one as well as possible. One way to do this is to look within your own heart, at the different facets of your personality. You may find a con man, an orphan, a nurse, a king, a hooker, a preacher, a loser, a child, a crone. Go into each of these people and try to capture how each one feels, thinks, talks, survives.

Another way to familiarize yourself with your characters is to base them partly on someone you know, a model from real life or a composite—your Uncle Edgar, but with the nervous tics and the odd smell of this guy you observed for ten minutes in line at the post office. Squint at these characters in your mind, and then start to paint them for us. Pages and pages of straight description, though, will probably wear us out. See if you can hear what they would say and how they would say it. One line of dialogue that rings true reveals character in a way that pages of description can't.

How would your main characters describe their current circumstances to a close friend, before and then after a few drinks? See if you can take dictation from them as they tell you who they think they are and what life has been like lately. Here is a passage by Andre Dubus that I always pass out to my students when we first begin to talk about character:

> *I love short stories because I believe they are the way we live. They are what our friends tell us, in their pain and joy, their passion and rage, their yearning and their cry against injustice. We can sit all night with our friend while he talks about the end of his marriage, and what we finally get is a collection of stories about passion, tenderness, misunderstanding, sorrow, money; those hours and days and moments when he was absolutely married, whether he and his wife were screaming at each other, or sulking around the house, or making love. While his marriage was dying, he was also working; spending evenings with friends, rearing children; but those are other stories. Which is why, days after hearing a painful story by a friend,*

we see him and say: How are you? We know that by now he may
have another story to tell, or he may be in the middle of one, and
we hope it is joyful.

Think of the basket of each character's life: what holds the
ectoplasm together—what are this person's routines, beliefs?
What little things would your characters write in their journals:
I ate this, I hate that, I did this, I took the dog for a long
walk, I chatted with my neighbor. This is all the stuff that
tethers them to the earth and to other people, all the stuff
that makes each character think that life sort of makes sense.

The basket is an apt image because of all the holes. How
aware is each character of how flimsy the basket really is? How
present are your people? Someone once said to me, "I am
trying to learn to stay in the now—not the last now, not the
next now; *this* now." Which "now" do your characters dwell
in?

What are your characters teaching their children by example
and by indoctrination? For instance, I was teaching Sam peace
chants for a long time, when he was only two. It was during
the war in the Persian Gulf; I was a little angry.

"What do we want?" I'd call to Sam.

"Peace," he'd shout dutifully.

"And when do we want it?" I'd ask.

"Now!" he'd say, and I'd smile and toss him a fish.

The words were utterly meaningless to him, of course. I
might as well have taught him to reply "Spoos!" instead of
"Peace" and "August!" instead of "Now." My friends loved

it, though; all three of his grandparents loved it. Now, how much does this say about me and my longings? I think something like this would tell a reader more about a character than would three pages of description. It would tell us about her current politics and the political tradition from which she sprang, her people-pleasing, her longing for peace and her longing to belong, her way of diluting rage and frustration with humor, while also using her child as a prop, a little live Charlie McCarthy. The latter is horrifying, but it's also sort of poignant. Maybe thirty-five years ago this woman had to perform for her parents' friends. Maybe she was their little Charlie McCarthy. Maybe she and her therapist can discuss it for the next few months. And did this woman stop using her kid, once she realized what she was doing? No, she didn't, and this tells us even more. She kept at it, long after the war was over, until one day she called to her three-and-a-half-year-old son, "Hey—what do we want?" And he said plaintively, "Lunch."

I once asked Ethan Canin to tell me the most valuable thing he knew about writing, and without hesitation he said, "Nothing is as important as a likable narrator. Nothing holds a story together better." I think he's right. If your narrator is someone whose take on things fascinates you, it isn't really going to matter if nothing much happens for a long time. I could watch John Cleese or Anthony Hopkins do dishes for about an hour without needing much else to happen. Having a likable narrator is like having a great friend whose company you love, whose mind you love to pick, whose running commentary totally holds your attention, who makes you laugh out loud, whose lines you always want to steal. When you have a friend like this, she can say, "Hey, I've got to drive up to the dump in Petaluma—wanna come along?" and you honestly can't think of anything in the world you'd rather do. By the same token, a boring or annoying person can offer to buy you an expensive dinner, followed by tickets to a great show, and in all honesty you'd rather stay home and watch the aspic set.

Now, a person's faults are largely what make him or her likable. I like for narrators to be like the people I choose for friends, which is to say that they have a lot of the same flaws as I. Preoccupation with self is good, as is a tendency toward procrastination, self-delusion, darkness, jealousy, groveling, greediness, addictiveness. They shouldn't be too perfect; perfect means shallow and unreal and fatally uninteresting. I like for them to have a nice sick sense of humor and to be concerned with important things, by which I mean that they are interested in political and psychological and spiritual matters. I want them to want to know who we are and what life is all about. I like them to be mentally ill in the same sorts of ways that I am; for instance, I have a friend who said one day, "I could resent the *ocean* if I tried," and I realized that I love that in a guy. I like for them to have hope—if a friend or a narrator reveals himself or herself to be hopeless too early on, I lose interest. It depresses me. It makes me overeat. I don't mind if a person has no hope if he or she is sufficiently funny about the whole thing, but then, this being able to be funny definitely speaks of a kind of hope, of buoyancy. Novels ought to have hope; at least, American novels ought to have hope. French novels don't need to. We mostly win wars, they lose them. Of course, they did hide more Jews than many other countries, and this is a form of winning. Although as my friend Jane points out, if you or I had been there speaking really bad French, they would have turned us in in a hot second—bank on it. In general, though, there's no point in writing hopeless novels. We all know we're going to die; what's important is the kind of men and women we are in the face of this.

Sometimes people turn out to be not all that funny or articulate, but they can still be great friends or narrators if they possess a certain clarity of vision—especially if they have survived or are in the process of surviving a great deal. This is inherently interesting material, since this is the task before all of us: sometimes we have to have one hand on this rock here, one hand on that one, and each big toe seeking out firm if temporary footing, and while we're scaling that rock face, there's no time for bubbles, champagne, and a witty aside. You don't mind that people in this situation are not being charming. You are glad to see them doing something you will need to do down the line, and with dignity. The challenge and the dignity make it interesting enough.

Besides, deciding what is interesting is about as subjective as things get. People hand me books and articles to read that they promise are fascinating, and I wake up holding the book, with a jerk—like when you wake up from a little nap at the movies, thinking that you are falling out of an airplane. Here,

for me, is the last word on interesting, from a short story by
Abigail Thomas:

> *My mother's first criterion for a man is that he be interesting. What*
> *this really means is that he be able to appreciate my mother, whose*
> *jokes hinge on some grammatical subtlety or a working knowledge*
> *of higher mathematics. You get the picture. Robbie is about as*
> *interesting as a pair of red high-top Converse sneakers. But Robbie*
> *points to the mattress on the floor. He grins, slowly unbuckling his*
> *belt, drops his jeans. "Lie down," says Robbie.*
>
> *This is interesting enough for me.*

Another thing: we want a sense that an important character,
like a narrator, is reliable. We want to believe that a character
is not playing games or being coy or manipulative, but is telling
the truth to the best of his or her ability. (Unless a major
characteristic of his or hers is coyness or manipulation or
lying.) We do not wish to be crudely manipulated. Of course,
we enter into a work of fiction to be manipulated, but in a
pleasurable way. We want to be massaged by a masseur, not
whapped by a carpet beater.

This brings us to the matter of how we, as writers, tell the
truth. A writer paradoxically seeks the truth and tells lies
every step of the way. It's a lie if you make something up.
But you make it up in the name of the truth, and then you
give your heart to expressing it clearly. You make up your
characters, partly from experience, partly out of the thin air
of the subconscious, and you need to feel committed to telling

the exact truth about them, even though you are making them up. I suppose the basic moral reason for doing this is the Golden Rule. I don't want to be lied to; I want you to tell me the truth, and I will try to tell it to you.

One final reminder: you probably won't know your characters until weeks or months after you've started working with them. Frederick Buechner wrote:

> *You avoid forcing your characters to march too steadily to the drumbeat of your artistic purpose. You leave some measure of real freedom for your characters to be themselves. And if minor characters show an inclination to become major characters, as they're apt to do, you at least give them a shot at it, because in the world of fiction it may take many pages before you find out who the major characters really are, just as in the real world it may take you many years to find out that the stranger you talked to once for half an hour in the railroad station may have done more to point you to where your true homeland lies than your priest or your best friend or even your psychiatrist.*

Just don't pretend you know more about your characters than they do, because you don't. Stay open to them. It's teatime and all the dolls are at the table. Listen. It's that simple.

Plot

Plot is the main story of your book or short story. If you are looking for long, brilliant discussions of plot, E. M. Forster and John Gardner have written books in which they discuss it so lucidly and wisely that they will leave you howling like a wolf. I just want to add a few thoughts here, things that I pass on to my students when they seem especially bitter and confused.

Plot grows out of character. If you focus on who the people in your story are, if you sit and write about two people you know and are getting to know better day by day, something is bound to happen.

Characters should not, conversely, serve as pawns for some plot you've dreamed up. Any plot you impose on your characters will be onomatopoetic: PLOT. I say don't worry about plot. Worry about the characters. Let what they say or do reveal who they are, and be involved in their lives, and keep asking yourself, Now what happens? The development of relationship creates plot. Flannery O'Connor, in *Mystery and Manners,* tells how she gave a bunch of her early stories to the old lady who lived down the street, and the woman returned them saying, "Them stories just gone and shown you how some folks *would* do."

That's what plot is: what people will up and do in spite of everything that tells them they shouldn't, everything that tells them that they should sit quietly on the couch and practice their Lamaze, or call their therapist, or eat until the urge to do that thing passes.

So focus on character. What happens in Faulkner's books, for instance, arises from the nature of his characters, and even though his characters are not necessarily people you want to date, they compel us because we believe that they exist and we believe that the things they do are true to who they are. We read Faulkner for the beauty of his horrible creations, the beauty of the writing, and we read him to find out what life is about from his point of view. He expresses this through his characters. All you can give us is what life is about from your point of view. You are not going to be able to give us the plans to the submarine. Life is not a submarine. There are no plans.

Find out what each character cares most about in the world because then you will have discovered what's at stake. Find a way to express this discovery in action, and then let your people set about finding or holding onto or defending whatever it is. Then you can take them from good to bad and back

again, or from bad to good, or from lost to found. But something must be at stake or you will have no tension and your
readers will not turn the pages. Think of a hockey player—
there had better be a puck out there on the ice, or he is going
to look pretty ridiculous.

This is how it works for me: I sit down in the morning and
reread the work I did the day before. And then I wool-gather,
staring at the blank page or off into space. I imagine my
characters, and let myself daydream about them. A movie
begins to play in my head, with emotion pulsing underneath
it, and I stare at it in a trancelike state, until words bounce
around together and form a sentence. Then I do the menial
work of getting it down on paper, because I'm the designated
typist, and I'm also the person whose job it is to hold the
lantern while the kid does the digging. What is the kid digging
for? The *stuff.* Details and clues and images, invention, fresh
ideas, an intuitive understanding of people. I tell you, the
holder of the lantern doesn't even know what the kid is digging
for half the time—but she knows gold when she sees it.

Your plot will fall into place as, one day at a time, you listen
to your characters carefully, and watch them move around
doing and saying things and bumping into each other. You'll
see them influence each other's lives, you'll see what they are
capable of up and doing, and you'll see them come to various
ends. And this process of discovering the story will often take
place in fits and starts. Don't worry about it. Keep trying to

move the story forward. There will be time later to render it in a smooth and seamless way. John Gardner wrote that the writer is creating a dream into which he or she invites the reader, and that the dream must be vivid and continuous. I tell my students to write this down—*that the dream must be vivid and continuous*—because it is so crucial. Outside the classroom, you don't get to sit next to your readers and explain little things you left out, or fill in details that would have made the action more interesting or believable. The material has got to work on its own, and the dream must be vivid and continuous. Think of your nightly dreams, how smoothly one scene slides into another, how you don't roll your closed eyes and say, "Wait just a minute—I've *never* shot drugs with Rosalyn Carter, and I don't even *own* any horses, let alone little Arabians the size of cats." You mostly go along from scene to scene simply because it's all so immediate and compelling. You simply *have* to find out what happens next, and this is how you want your reader to feel.

You may need someone else to bounce your material off of, probably a friend or a mate, someone who can tell you if the seams show, or if you've lurched off track, or even that it is not as bad as you thought and that the first one hundred pages do in fact hold up. But by all means let someone else take a look at your work. It's too hard always to have to be the executioner. Also, you may not be able to see the problems, because in finding your characters and their story, you are trying to describe something by feel and not by sight. So find someone who can bring a colder eye and a certain detachment to the project. I had a friend named Al who every so often took other people's cats to the pound to be put down, because his friends couldn't bear to do it themselves. They were cats who were, for one reason or another, like sickness or incontinence, a blight on the landscape. He didn't care one way or the other about cats. He had an imaginary company, whose business was having cats put to sleep, whose slogan was "The pussy must pay." Let someone do this with your manuscripts, help you get rid of the twists in the plot that are never going to work no matter how hard you try or how many passes you make at it.

If I tell thirty students to write me a story about two married people who are considering divorce until something unforeseen happens, they'll give me thirty wildly different stories, because they will have thirty different personal histories and sensibilities. One person is going to write an epiphany story, where the wife sees some wild geese pass in the night, lit by the moon, and suddenly decides to give her husband another chance. Another person is going to write about the moment when the husband, on his morning run, first comes to believe his marriage is worth saving and then is jogging home to share the good news with his wife when he gets hit by a student driver. Another will set the story in Hollywood, because he's been reading Nathanael West recently, and it will be jewellike in its weirdness. Each writer will come up with his or her own description of what love and life are all about. Some of these descriptions will be cynical, some rueful, some full of hope. Some will be slow and interior, some will crackle with drama.

Drama is the way of holding the reader's attention. The basic formula for drama is setup, buildup, payoff—just like a joke. The setup tells us what the game is. The buildup is where you put in all the moves, the forward motion, where you get all the meat off the turkey. The payoff answers the question, Why are we here anyway? What is it that you've been trying to give? Drama must move forward and upward, or the seats on which the audience is sitting will become very hard and uncomfortable. So, in fact, will the audience. And eventually the audience will become impatient, disappointed, and unhappy. There must be movement.

You need to be moving your characters forward, even if they only go slowly. Imagine moving them across a lily pond. If each lily pad is beautifully, carefully written, the reader will stay with you as you move toward the other side of the pond, needing only the barest of connections—such as rhythm, tone, or mood.

Now, you may have to use effects and tricks to move things along and to help us remember who each character is—give him a cigar, give her piggy little alcoholic eyes—but if you're faking it, it will show. If you knowingly fake something to get the plot to move forward—if, for instance, you have taken a character you don't understand and given her feelings you don't really feel because you want the plot to work—you probably won't get away with it. The reader will stop trusting you and will possibly even become bitter and resentful. These are the worst possible things for a reader to become. You must assume that we, your readers, are bright and attentive, even if we have lost the tiniest bit of ground in the last few years. So we are going to catch you if you try to fake it.

If you realize that you have done this, you need to stop and look at your characters again. You've got to go into these people, and since you don't know them, this means that you need to go into you, wonderful you, who has so many problems and idiosyncrasies—you, who will be able to figure out what is true for these people and hence, what they would or would not do in a given situation.

I read a wonderful passage in an interview with Carolyn Chute, the author of *The Beans of Egypt, Maine,* who was discussing rewriting: "I feel like a lot of time my writing is like having about twenty boxes of Christmas decorations. But no tree. You're going, Where do I put this? Then they go, Okay, you can have a tree, but we'll blindfold you and you gotta cut it down with a spoon." This is how I've arrived at my plots a number of times. I would have all these wonderful shiny bulbs, each self-contained with nothing to hang them on. But I would stay with the characters, caring for them, getting to know them better and better, suiting up each morning and working as hard as I could, and somehow, mysteriously, I would come to know what their story was. Over and over I feel as if my characters know who they are, and what happens to them, and where they have been and where they will go, and what they are capable of doing, but they need me to write it down for them because their handwriting is so bad.

Some writers claim to know what the climax is early on, well before they get anywhere near it. The climax is that major event, usually toward the end, that brings all the tunes you have been playing so far into one major chord, after which at least one of your people is profoundly changed. If someone isn't changed, then what is the point of your story? For the climax, there must be a killing or a healing or a domination. It can be a real killing, a murder, or it can be a killing of the spirit, or of something terrible inside one's soul, or it can be a killing of a deadness within, after which the person becomes alive again. The healing may be about union, reclamation, the rescue of a fragile prize. But whatever happens, we need to feel that it was inevitable, that even though we may be amazed, it feels absolutely right, that of course things would come to this, of course they would shake down in this way.

In order to have this sense of inevitability, the climax of your story will probably only reveal itself to you slowly and over time. You may think that you know what this moment contains—and it makes sense to aim for something—but I recommend that you not fix too hard on what it will be. Fix instead on who your people are and how they feel toward one another, what they say, how they smell, whom they fear.

Let your human beings follow the music they hear, and let it take them where it will. Then you may discover, when you get close enough to peer into the opening, as if into a scenic Easter egg, that your characters had something in mind all along that was brighter and much more meaningful than what you wanted to impose on them.

So aim but not too hard, and when you finally see the climax forming in front of you, *then* you can race toward it.

Lastly: I heard Alice Adams give a lecture on the short story once, one aspect of which made the writing students in her audience so excited that I have passed it along to my students ever since. (Most of the time I give her credit.) She said that sometimes she uses a formula when writing a short story, which goes ABDCE, for Action, Background, Development, Climax, and Ending. You begin with action that is compelling enough to draw us in, make us want to know more. Background is where you let us see and know who these people are, how they've come to be together, what was going on before the opening of the story. Then you develop these people, so that we learn what they care most about. The plot—the drama, the actions, the tension—will grow out of that. You move them along until everything comes together in the climax, after which things are different for the main characters, different in some real way. And then there is the ending: what is our sense of who these people are now, what are they left with, what happened, and what did it mean?

A formula can be a great way to get started. And it feels

so great finally to dive into the water; maybe you splash around and flail for a while, but at least you're in. Then you start doing whatever stroke you can remember how to do, and you get this scared feeling inside you—of how hard it is and how far there is to go—but still you're in, and you're afloat, and you're moving.

Dialogue

Good dialogue is such a pleasure to come across while reading, a complete change of pace from description and exposition and all that *writing*. Suddenly people are talking, and we find ourselves clipping along. And we have all the pleasures of voyeurism because the characters don't know we are listening. We get to feel privy to their inner workings without having to spend too much time listening to them think. I don't want them to think all the time on paper. It's bad enough that *I* have to think all the time without having someone else dump his or her obsessive-compulsive, paranoid thinking on me, too.

On the other hand, nothing can break the mood of a piece of writing like bad dialogue. My students are miserable when they are reading an otherwise terrific story to the class and then hit a patch of dialogue that is so purple and expositional that it reads like something from a childhood play by the Gabor sisters. Suddenly the piece is emotionally tone-deaf and there's a total lack of resonance. I can see the surprise on my students' faces, because the dialogue looked Okay on paper, yet now it sounds as if it were poorly translated from their native Hindi. The problem is that the writer simply put it down word by word; read out loud, it has no flow, no sense of the character's rhythm that in real life would run through the words.

In nonfiction, the hope is that the person actually said the words that you have attributed to him or her. In fiction, though, anything goes. It is a matter of ear, just as finding the right physical detail is mostly a matter of eye. You're not reproducing actual speech—you're translating the sound and rhythm of what a character says into words. You're putting down on paper your sense of how the characters speak.

There is a real skill to hearing all those words that real people—and your characters—say and to recording what you have heard—and the latter is or should be more interesting and concise and even more true than what was actually said. Dialogue is more like a movie than it is like real life, since it should be more dramatic. There's a greater sense of action. In the old days, before movies, let's say before Hemingway, the dialogue in novels was much more studied, ornate. Characters talked in ways we can't really imagine people talking. With Hemingway, things began to terse up. Good dialogue became sharp and lean. Now, in the right hands, dialogue can move things along in a way that will leave you breathless.

There are a number of things that help when you sit down to write dialogue. First of all, sound your words—read them out loud. If you can't bring yourself to do this, mouth your dialogue. This is something you have to practice, doing it over and over and over. Then when you're out in the world—that is, not at your desk—and you hear people talking, you'll find yourself editing their dialogue, playing with it, seeing in your mind's eye what it would look like on the page. You listen to how people really talk, and then learn little by little to take someone's five-minute speech and make it one sentence, without losing anything. If you are a writer, or want to be a writer, this is how you spend your days—listening, observing, storing things away, making your isolation pay off. You take home all you've taken in, all that you've overheard, and you turn it into gold. (Or at least you try.)

Second, remember that you should be able to identify each character by what he or she says. Each one must sound different from the others. And they should not all sound like you; each one must have a self. If you can get their speech mannerisms right, you will know what they're wearing and driving and maybe thinking, and how they were raised, and what they feel. You need to trust yourself to hear what *they* are saying over what you are saying. At least give each of them a shot at expression: sometimes what they are saying and how they are saying it will finally show you who they are and what is really happening. Whoa—they're not going to get married after all! She's gay! And you had no idea!

Third, you might want to try putting together two people who more than anything else in the world wish to avoid each other, people who would avoid whole cities just to make sure they won't bump into each other. But there are people out there in the world who almost inspire me to join the government witness protection program, just so I can be sure I will never have to talk to them again. Maybe there is someone like this in your life. Take a character whom one of your main characters feels this way about and put the two of them in the same elevator. Then let the elevator get stuck. Nothing like a supercharged atmosphere to get things going. Now, they both will have a lot to say, but they will also be afraid that they won't be able to control *what* they say. They will be afraid of an explosion. Maybe there will be one, maybe not. But there's one way to find out. In any case, good dialogue gives us the sense that we are eavesdropping, that the author is not getting in the way. Thus, good dialogue encompasses both what is said and what is not said. What is not said will sit patiently outside that stuck elevator door, or it will dart around the characters' feet inside the elevator, like rats. So let these characters hold back some thoughts, and at the same time, let them detonate little bombs.

If you are lucky, your characters may become impatient with your inability, while writing dialogue, to keep up with all they have to say. This is when you will know that you are on the right track.

Dialogue is *the* way to nail character, so you have to work on getting the voice right. You don't want to sit there, though, trying to put the right words in their mouths. I don't think the right words exist already in your head, any more than the characters do. They exist somewhere else. What we have in our heads are fragments and thoughts and things we've heard and memorized, and we take our little ragbag and reach into it and throw some stuff down and then our unconscious kicks in. For instance, say you have a guy walking down the street, and it's cold, and you've always wanted a leather topcoat, so you give him one. Then you follow him down the street. Describe what you see, and listen carefully.

Say this boy meets a girl. The boy in the leather overcoat meets the beautiful girl with the harelip and the Gucci bag, on the street, and he can't just say, Hey, let's get married! Things need to happen. They need to get to know each other, even if just a little. They will talk to each other, and they will talk about each other to friends. Get all this down. After you've spent a while with them, they will start to sound more like themselves—because you are getting to really know them—and you may see that you'd better get rid of that topcoat, it's pretty jive, and that you need to go back and redo the early dialogue. But don't stop and do it just now. Keep moving; let them spend some time together, let them jam for a while. Come back later for the rewrite.

The better you know the characters, the more you'll see things from their point of view. You need to trust that you've got it in you to listen to people, watch them, and notice what they wear and how they move, to capture a sense of how they speak. You want to avoid at all costs drawing your characters on those that already exist in other works of fiction. You must learn about people from people, not from what you read. Your reading should *confirm* what you've observed in the world.

As you learn who your characters are, compassion for them will grow. There shouldn't be just a single important character in your work for whom you have compassion. You need to feel it even for the villain—in fact, especially for the villain. Life is not like formula fiction. The villain has a heart, and the hero has great flaws. You've got to pay attention to what each character says, so you can know each of their hearts.

Only in the comics and formula movies do we get any pleasure from destroying totally evil and sinister villains, because in those cases they've been systematically depersonalized. They commit only acts of atrocity and sociopathology, and they say terribly evil things, and then we get to ritually kill them. There can be, at the end of the book, the relief that comes with justice.

You can't write down your intellectual understanding of a hero or villain and expect us to be engaged. You probably have got to find these characters within the community of people who live in your heart. For instance, just to mix media for a moment, if Anthony Hopkins in *The Silence of the Lambs* hadn't had an emotional understanding of Hannibal Lector's heart, his mannerisms would not have rung so true or been so terrifying. The first time we see him, he's simply standing there, expressionless, with his arms by his side. It is just chilling. I felt like I might break out in welts from sheer anxiety. I felt like my neck had developed a life of its own and was going to wait for me out in the lobby. To have this effect on us, Hopkins must have sympathized with something inside Lector, must have understood something about his heart.

The writer needs to try to understand each of his or her characters in this way. The only thing to do when the sense of dread and low self-esteem tells you that you are not up to this is to wear it down by getting a little work done every day. You really can do it, really can find these people inside you and learn to hear what they have to say.

For example, let's say you have a main character whose feelings can be hurt if he's spoken to sharply—unlike you, ha-ha-ha. Say he is also a little like you in the sense that when he gets a bit depressed or tense, he heads for a rib joint to eat a pound of burned, fatty meat. So he is perhaps also a little overweight—not that you are overweight. I'm sure your weight is just fine. *Anyway,* let's make him someone who works in an office, someone who's been pampered—what could he say that lets us see this? Let's dress him carefully because we may have to humiliate him in a minute. For instance, we can see by the precision of the knot in his tie that his wife tied it this morning. His clothes and ring and shoes are all going to talk, and they are going to help us find out who he is, but more importantly he is going to say things to his secretary and to his callers and to the people with whom he works, and these people are going to say things back to him, and we want to hear both sides of these conversations.

What if his boss says something to him that seems innocuous but that cuts him to the quick? And what if this time he responds in a completely different way than heading out for barbecue? What if he starts saying things that have nothing to do with what *you* had in mind, and it all mysteriously rings true? What if he says something so insulting to his boss that it puts his job in jeopardy, and then, instead of a little assault eating, he responds by spending his entire lunch hour at an adult bookstore? Well, maybe you had him wrong to begin with. Maybe he goes from being an Ivy League lawyer to a semisuccessful rug salesman in two lines of dialogue. This may not be convenient for you, but at least now you can see with whom you are really working.

Now I want to hear how he describes his day to his wife, what he leaves in and how he says it, and what he neglects to mention. So you make an attempt at capturing this by trying to find him in your psyche, this person who has been talked down to, whose skin is a little thin, whose feelings are easily hurt. You write a shitty first draft of it and you sound it out, and you leave in those lines that ring true and take out the rest. I wish there were an easier, softer way, a shortcut, but this is the nature of most good writing: that you find out things as you go along. Then you go back and rewrite. Remember: no one is reading your first drafts.

I need to digress again for a minute: you create these characters and figure out little by little what they say and do, but this all happens in a part of you to which you have no access—the unconscious. This is where the creating is done. We start out with stock characters, and our unconscious provides us with real, flesh-and-blood, believable people. My friend Carpenter talks about the unconscious as the cellar where the little boy sits who creates the characters, and he hands them up to you through the cellar door. He might as well be cutting out paper dolls. He's peaceful; he's just playing.

You can't will yourself into being receptive to what the little boy has to offer, and you can't buy a key that will let you into the cellar. You have to relax, and wool-gather, and get rid of the critics, and sit there in some sort of self-hypnosis, and then you have to *practice*. I mean, you can't just sit there at your desk drooling. You have to move your hand across the paper or the keyboard. You may do it badly for a while, but you keep on doing it. Try to remember that to some extent, you're just the typist. A good typist listens.

I sometimes imagine that instead of a little kid, there's a long-necked, good-natured Dr. Seuss character down there, grim with concentration and at the same time playing. He cranes his head toward the sound of the characters talking, but not like a court reporter, more like somebody sitting alone at an adjacent table, trying not to pry but wanting to take it all in. You may want to come up with an image or a metaphor for this other part of you that is separate from your rational, conscious mind, this other person with whom you can collaborate. This may help you feel less alone.

One last thing: dialogue that is written in dialect is very tiring to read. If you can do it brilliantly, fine. If other writers read your work and rave about your use of dialect, go for it. But be positive that you do it well, because otherwise it is a lot of work to read short stories or novels that are written in dialect. It makes our necks feel funny. We are, as you know, a tense people, and we have a lot of problems of our own without you adding to them. (However, someone behind me in line at the market last week, during a storm, said, after smiting her own forehead, "Oh, vat vader," and then pointed outside to the rain. I was tempted for the rest of the day to write an entire novel about her, in dialect.)

Set Design

Sometimes you may find it useful to let your characters huddle in the wings without you, preparing for their roles, improvising dialogue, while you set the stage for their appearance. Imagine yourself as the set designer for a play or for the movie version of the story you are working on. It may help you to know what the room (or the ship or the office or the meadow) looks like where the action will be taking place. You want to know its feel, its temperature, its colors. Just as everyone is a walking advertisement for who he or she is, so every room is a little showcase of its occupants' values and personalities. Every room is about memory. Every room gives us layers of information about our past and present and who we are, our shrines and quirks and hopes and sorrows, our attempts to prove that we exist and are more or less Okay. You can see, in our rooms, how much light we need—how many light bulbs, candles, skylights we have—and in how we keep things lit you can see how we try to comfort ourselves. The mix in our rooms is so touching: the clutter and the cracks in the wall belie a bleakness or brokenness in our lives, while photos and a few rare objects show our pride, our rare shining moments.

As the photographer Catherine Wagner has pointed out, these rooms are future ruins.

So you sit there at your desk trying to see what the set looks like that your characters will be entering in a moment. Perhaps they have money and you don't—not, of course, that you're bitter about this. You may need to call one of your friends or relatives who has or had a great deal of money, and ask them as tactfully as possible to help you design a house where some old gentry lived. By tactfully, I mean that you're going to get the best possible information if you do not mention life's unfairness and that your own house looks more like *God's Little Acre* with every passing day and that you may have to put the dog to sleep because you can't afford to feed her. You just say, "I'm working on a section of my book where we first meet a family of great wealth and breeding, and I was wondering if I could pick your brain about what sort of carpets and rugs and lighting and antiques they might have. For instance, let's start with the living room. Can you describe a really lovely living room in as much detail as possible?" And then you can ask what smells your friend remembers, in the living room and kitchen, and what the light was like, and what various rooms sounded like or what their silences felt like. Or by the same token, you can ask someone who grew up in poverty to give you an exact description of his or her house, the kitchen, the bedrooms, the couch in the backyard.

Years ago I was working on a novel that involved a woman who gardened, who in fact loved to garden. I do not love to garden. I love other people's gardens, and I like cut flowers. I have Astroturf and a whole lot of high-quality plastic flowers stuck in the dirt of our front yard. These are quite a lovely sight and bring to mind many e. e. cummings poems.

People used to give me potted plants and trees, and what happened to them is really too horrible to go into here. They'd end up looking like I watered them with Agent Orange. I'd tell people that I didn't do well with potted plants, and they'd decide that I'd just never met the right one and that they were going to be the person to free me and cause God to restore my glorious gift of sight and all that, and they'd bring me some little training plant, and I'd try really hard to water it and keep it in or out of sunlight, whatever its little card of introduction said it preferred, and to take it for little walks around the house, and within about a month you could almost hear chlorophyllous breakdown, a *Panic in Needle Park* sort of thing. Then you'd see it clutching its little throat, staring at you with its little Keane eyes, gasping and accusing—and I mean, who needs it? Believe me, I have enough problems as it is.

I actually kept this one horrible plant alive for months, this huge potted thing. I don't even know what it was, but it was about three feet tall, before its decline, and green in a sort of fake jolly way. I watered it, I cut off its dead leaves, and how did it repay me? By becoming Howard Hughes in his last days. It lost all this weight, it stopped going out. I came to believe that it would be requesting latex gloves soon, boxes of them, and boxes of Kleenex with which to cover its food between bites. I gave it water, sunlight, expensive plant food—what was I supposed to do, get it a psychiatrist? So I finally came to my senses, took it outside, and put it against the side of the house where I wouldn't have to look at it. You are probably thinking that it immediately began to flourish, but it didn't. It died.

So, needless to say, when it came time to design a garden for my main character, I wasn't going to be able to plumb the depths of my own gardening experience. But I just knew somehow, without being able to explain the process to you, that this main character gardened. I love to see people in gardens, I love the meditation of sitting alone in gardens, I love all the metaphors that gardens are.

The garden is one of the two great metaphors for humanity. The other, of course, is the river. Metaphors are a great language tool, because they explain the unknown in terms of the known. But they only work if they resonate in the heart of the writer. So I felt a little understaffed here, loving the metaphor when I came upon it, wanting to work with it, and yet not loving to garden.

I didn't know where to start, but I did know that the garden did not start out as metaphor. It started out as paradise. Then, as now, the garden is about life and beauty and the impermanence of all living things. The garden is about feeding your children, providing food for the tribe. It's part of an urgent territorial drive that we can probably trace back to animals storing food. It's a competitive display mechanism, like having a prize bull, this greed for the best tomatoes and English tea roses; it's about winning, about providing society with superior things, and about proving that you have taste and good values and you work hard. And what a wonderful relief every so often to know who the enemy is—because in the garden, the enemy is everything: the aphids, the weather, time. And so you pour yourself into it, care so much, and see up close so much birth and growth and beauty and danger and triumph—and then everything dies anyway, right? But you just keep doing it. What a great metaphor! I love this so much! I wanted a garden in my book so badly! Finally, finally, it occurred to me to call a nursery.

I reached a very nice man to whom I explained what I was doing, and I asked if he could help me design a fictional garden for someone living in the North Bay with a large backyard.

We decided to begin by showing the garden as it would look in the summer, and then he would help me through the months as the seasons changed.

"Do you want some fruit trees?" he asked.

And then for the next half hour, we designed a garden full of trees and flowers of every kind. I said I saw in my mind's eye a white latticework screen somewhere in the garden, and asked what kinds of vines might go well with that. He suggested snow peas. Then we added some vegetables, and a patch of wild strawberries, and I had my garden. I got into the habit of calling him every few months to check in. "What would the apple tree be doing?" I'd ask. "Would there be fruit, or even leaves? And what would I do to take care of the flower beds now?"

I also started going to people's gardens, asking them what this or that plant was and how they take care of it, and they'd say funny or brilliant things and I'd steal their lines. I picked up a book on gardens, so I could study flowers and trees and vines in that way, and honest to God, people who read my novel believed that I loved to garden. Sometimes in fact they would start talking shop with me, thinking we could jam away, as gardeners are wont to do, until I'd let them know that I had only been winging it, with a lot of help from people around me, people who knew a lot more about gardens than I, friends who would cover for me, just like in real life.

"You don't love to garden?" they'd ask incredulously, and I'd shake my head and not mention that what I love are cut flowers, because this sounds so violent and decadent, like when Salvador Dalí said his favorite animal was fillet of sole.

And in the years since, I have asked all sorts of people to help me design sets. I've asked them to describe what the world looked like in certain American cities or African villages, inside a particular car in the rain, or down by the water when hoboes still came to town on the train. Then I try to imagine the movie set of this scene in as much detail as possible. Sometimes I can see it most clearly if I close my eyes. Other times I stare off into the middle distance, like a cat.

F a l s e   S t a r t s

I talked earlier about the artist who is trying to capture something in one corner of his canvas but keeps discovering that what he has painted is not what he had in mind. He keeps covering his work over with white paint each time that he discovers what it isn't, and each time this brings him closer to discovering what it is. This has happened again and again for me in writing. I may think I know who a certain character is or how an essay should proceed, so I make a stab at following this ghostly blueprint in my head. Then it turns out that I've been wrong, wrong about the character. I had the sandwich board she was wearing confused with who she really is. So I white it out and try again.

I found out something important about false starts when I began accompanying some members of my church to a convalescent home once a month, where we were conducting a worship service. After that first dismal visit, I thought I knew who the residents were and what they were capable of, what they were all about. If I had started to write, I would have written about them with confidence, and I would have been all wrong.

I have been going there for four years now. I don't ever really look forward to it, but I keep going back for reasons I do not quite understand. Perhaps I am subconsciously hoping it will help me get into the Junior League someday. Still, the moment I walk in and smell those old people again, and find them parked in the hallways like so many cars abandoned by the side of the road, I start begging God not to let me end up like this. But God is not a short-order cook, and these people were once my age. I bet they used to beg God not to let them end up as they have.

At first many of them look strangely alike, just as many people at the Special Olympics bear a familial resemblance to one another. Then you start to notice that some have lambskin chaps or blankets, some have manicures, some have the teeth they were born with, some have sores, some don't, some were clearly beautiful in earlier days, some weren't, some seem to know where they are, some remember lines from the Lord's Prayer, some sleep, some try to sing along on the simple hymns and clap in rhythm. But even the ones who clap all clap differently. Some clap along frailly, almost in silence. One woman claps with great gusto, as if she's at a polka. One old man claps once, as if to kill a fly. My favorite, a woman named Anne like me, is someone I'd first pegged as a muzzy, emaciated woman who smelled of urine and baby powder without a whole lot going on inside. She isn't what I thought, though. I still don't know who she is, but I do know now who she isn't.

She can never remember my name, and when I tell her every month, she pantomimes smiting her own forehead. Then we both smile. I suspect she is pulling my leg. When we sing "Amen," she always sits with her hands in her lap, palms cupped together as if there might be a tiny bird inside. With each clap, she moves her hands a tiny bit apart, as if she really does want to clap along, but at the same time she doesn't want to let the bird get out.

If I'd written about her and the other old people after the first few visits, the smells and confusion would have dominated my description. I would have recorded our odd conversations—one woman is convinced we went to school together; another once asked if Sam was a dog—and I would have tried to capture my sense of waste. Instead, I continued to go there, and I struggled to find meaning in their bleak existence. What finally helped was an image from a medieval monk, Brother Lawrence, who saw all of us as trees in winter, with little to give, stripped of leaves and color and growth, whom God loves unconditionally *anyway.* My priest friend Margaret, who works with the aged and who shared this image with me, wanted me to see that even though these old people are no longer useful in any traditional meaning of the word, they are there to be loved unconditionally, like trees in the winter.

When you write about your characters, we want to know all about their leaves and colors and growth. But we also want to know who they are when stripped of the surface show. So if you want to get to know your characters, you have to hang out with them long enough to see beyond all the things they aren't. You may try to get them to do something because it would be convenient plotwise, or you might want to pigeon-hole them so you can maintain the illusion of control. But with luck their tendrils will sneak out the sides of the box you've put them in, and you will finally have to admit that who they are isn't who you thought they were.

Dying people can teach us this most directly. Often the attributes that define them drop away—the hair, the shape, the skills, the cleverness. And then it turns out that the packaging is not who that person has really been all along. Without the package, another sort of beauty shines through. For instance, on a retail-therapy outing ten days before she died, my friend Pammy discovered that she could no longer write her name on checks, and she turned to me and said, "What is the point of being alive when you can't even sign checks?" I could only shrug and shake my head. But it turned out that the essence of Pammy wasn't about the things she could do with her hands. Who she was wasn't about doing at all.

On the first anniversary of her death, I visited a memorial garden at the radiation clinic where she had been treated, and discovered that someone had planted a yew tree there in her honor. The yew was bigger than me and fuzzy, like an Edward Koren character. It looked like it might suddenly come over and hug me. Near the yew were tall flowering bushes—some kind of poppy, perhaps. But almost all of the petals had fallen off, so mostly I just saw a thousand tangled stems growing skyward. Then I realized that the stems were actually connected, and that they bore seeds that would flower again in the spring.

That's how real life works, in our daily lives as well as in the convalescent home and even at the deathbed, and this is what good writing allows us to notice sometimes. You can see the underlying essence only when you strip away the busyness, and then some surprising connections appear.

Plot Treatment

My students assume that when well-respected writers sit down to write their books, they know pretty much what is going to happen because they've outlined most of the plot, and this is why their books turn out so beautifully and why their lives are so easy and joyful, their self-esteem so great, their childlike senses of trust and wonder so intact. Well. I do not know anyone fitting this description at all. Everyone I know flails around, kvetching and growing despondent, on the way to finding a plot and structure that work. You are welcome to join the club.

On the other hand, in lieu of a plot you may find that you have a sort of temporary destination, perhaps a scene that you envision as the climax. So you write toward this scene, but when you get there, or close, you see that because of all you've learned about your characters along the way, it no longer works. The scene may have triggered the confidence that got you to work on your piece, but now it doesn't ring true and so it does not make the final cut.

I went through this process with my second novel, where an image kept me going while I came to have a strong sense of the people I was writing about. Yet when it was that climactic image's turn on the dance floor, it was all wrong. So I got very quiet for a few days and waited for the characters to come to me with their lines and intentions. Gradually I came to feel that I knew how the book ended, how it all hung together. By then, I had spent two solid years on the book, sending it off chunk by chunk to my editor at Viking.

My editor had loved the characters all along, had loved the tone and the writing, but after reading my finished second draft straight through, he sent me back a letter that began, "This is perhaps the hardest letter I've ever had to write." I saw stars right there at the post office, as if someone had hit me on the head. The room spun. The editor went on to say that while he enjoyed the people and what they had to say, I had in effect created a beautiful banquet but never invited the reader to sit down and eat. So the reader went hungry. And that, to mix metaphors, the book felt like a house with no foundation, no support beams, which was collapsing in on itself, and there was no way to shore it up. I should put it away and get to work on another book from scratch.

The thing is, I had already spent most of the advance.

I went into a very deep state of grief and fear at the post office, and this stuck with me for the next week or so. I was wild with humiliation and deeply afraid for my future. But I called someone who loved my writing, who had encouraged me all along, and she told me to give the book a little space, a little sunshine and fresh air. She said not to pick it up again for a month. She said that everything was going to be Okay, although she did not know exactly what Okay might look like.

So I went off to the elephants' graveyard, renting a room in a huge old house on the Petaluma River. It was very quiet and pastoral. No one knew who I was. Hardly anyone knew where I was. The meadows outside my windows were filled with cows and grass and hay. I licked my wounds for a couple of weeks and waited for my confidence to return. I tried not to make any big decisions about how to salvage the book or my writing life, because the one thing I knew for sure was that if you want to make God laugh, tell her your plans.

Finally, I found myself ready to look at the book again. I read it through in one sitting and loved it. I thought it was wonderful. A huge mess, granted, but a wonderful mess.

I called my editor and told him I knew what I was doing now and that I would prove this to him. He was genuinely happy.

There was a huge dilapidated living room in the house where I lived, and one morning I took my three-hundred-page manuscript and began to lay it down on the floor, section by section. I put a two-page scene here, a ten-page passage there. I put these pages down in a path, from beginning to end, like a horizontal line of dominoes, or like a garden path made of tiles. There were sections up front that clearly belonged in the middle, there were scenes in the last fifty pages that would be wonderful near the beginning, there were scenes and moments scattered throughout that could be collected and rewritten to make a great introduction to the two main characters. I walked up and down the path, moving batches of paper around, paper-clipping self-contained sections and scribbling notes to myself on how to shape or tighten or expand each section in whatever necessary way. I noticed where things were missing—transitions, vital information we needed to know before what happened could make any sense—and then, on a blank piece of paper, I blocked in what I thought was needed and lay the page on the pile where it fit in. This page held some space, perhaps for whole scenes, in the way that—after a loss—a great friend holds some space for you in which to grieve or find your bearings. Scribbling notes on various sections to indicate that in fact something was at stake there, I went ahead and let bad things happen to these people whom I had been protecting. I found places where I could lean on them harder, push them, load them up in a way that would make their catastrophe inevitable, and I blocked the catastrophe in, too. Then, when I was sure, I stacked up all the pages in their new order and set about writing a third draft.

I wrote that draft short assignment by short assignment, making each section, no matter how small or seemingly casual, as good as I could. I took out whole paragraphs that I loved, paragraphs I'd shoehorned into the book because I liked the writing or the image or the humor. I worked on it for eight or nine months, sending off the first third, which my editor was amazed by, and then the second section, which he loved.

I finished the third section around the time I broke up with a man with whom I'd been involved for some time. I had a brainstorm: I would mail the third section off, borrow the money to fly to New York, and spend a week there, doing the line editing of the book with my editor and, at the same time, getting away from this man I was breaking up with. Also, I could collect the last third of the advance that Viking owed me and do a little retail therapy in New York City.

I wrote to my editor to say I was coming. He did not say not to. I told the man I was involved with to move all of his stuff out of the house. I borrowed a thousand dollars from my aunt, promising her that I would pay it back by the end of the month. And then I flew to New York.

My first morning there, I put on my girl-writer dress and heels and went to meet my editor. I figured we would start editing together that very morning, and then he could give me the last of the advance. It would turn out that I had bounced back from this devastating setback and that truth and beauty had once again triumphed. Everyone would be so shocked to hear that this book had almost been thrown away. But my editor said, "I'm sorry." I looked at him quizzically. "I am so, so sorry," he said. "But it still doesn't work." He didn't understand why certain things happened the way they did, or why some things happened to begin with, and most importantly, why so little happened at all. I sat there staring at him as if his face were melting. "I am so sorry," he said, and for a while I was too stunned to cry. I kept touching my forehead, the way you pat your head to make sure your hair is Okay. I think I must have looked like Blanche DuBois on bad acid. Then I started to cry and told him I had to go right that very second. He said to phone him the next day. I said I would, although I did not actually expect to be alive then.

Luckily, I was still drinking at the time. I went to the house where I was staying with old family friends, slammed down a dozen social drinks with them, and then took a cab to meet some other friends. I had a few hundred more drinks with them, and the merest bit of cocaine—actually, I began to resemble an anteater at one point. Then I went to a liquor store and got a half-pint of Irish whiskey and went back to the house where I was staying and had little social slugs of Bushmills straight from the bottle until I passed out.

I was a little depressed when I woke up. I looked at my manuscript in my suitcase, thought about all those beautiful, hilarious, poignant people I had been working with for almost three years, and all of a sudden I was in a rage. I called my editor at home. He was not planning on going to work that day. He was a little depressed, too. "I am coming over," I said, and there was a silence, and then he said, very tentatively, "Okay," like he wanted to ask, "And will you be bringing your knives?" Then I went downstairs and caught a cab to his apartment.

He let me in and tried to get me to sit down, but I was too crazy and disappointed and angry and crushed and hu-miliated and shocked. I held my manuscript to my chest like a baby. There were sections where friends who had read it had laughed out loud, or had called me, crying. There was some incredibly funny material in there, some important things no one else was writing about. I was sure of it. Sort of. I began to stalk around his living room, like a trial lawyer making her case to the jury, explaining various aspects of the book, some of which, in my desire not to appear too obvious, I had forgotten to put down at all. I filled in lots of spaces, describing things that existed between the characters that I had assumed were clear. I was ranting—twenty-eight years old, savagely hung over, feeling like I was about to die—but I told him who the people were and what the story was. I sketched in the underpinnings of their lives and thought out loud how I could solve the bigger problems of plot and theme, how I could simplify some things and deepen others. I was not thinking about what I was going to say. Words were just pouring out of me, and when I was done, he looked at me, and said, "Thank you."

We sat side by side on his couch for a while, in silence. Finally he said, "Listen. I want you to write that book you just described to me. You haven't done it here. Go off somewhere and write me a treatment, a plot treatment. Tell me chapter by chapter what you just told me in the last half hour, and I will get you the last of the advance."

And I did. I arranged to stay with some friends in Cambridge for a month, and there I sat down every day and wrote five hundred to a thousand words describing what was going on in each chapter. I discussed who the characters were turning out to be, where they'd been, what they were up to, and why. I quoted directly from the manuscript sometimes, using some of the best lines to instill confidence in both me and my editor, and I figured out, over and over, point A, where the chapter began, and point B, where it ended, and what needed to happen to get my people from A to B. And then how the B of the last chapter would lead organically into point A of the next chapter. The book moved along like the alphabet, like a vivid and continuous dream. The treatment was forty pages long. I mailed it from Cambridge, and flew home.

It worked. My editor gave me the last of the advance, which I used to pay back my aunt and to buy time so I could write a final draft. This time I knew exactly what I was doing. I had a recipe. The book came out the following autumn and has been the most successful of my novels.

Whenever I tell this story to my students, they want to see the actual manuscript of the plot treatment. When I bring it in, they pore over it like it is some kind of Rosetta stone. It is typed on paper that has become crisp with age. There are annotations, smudges, and rings left by coffee and by red wine. It strikes me as being a brave document, rather like the little engine who could on the morning after.

How Do You Know When You're Done?

This is a question my students always ask. I don't quite know how to answer it. You just do. I think my students believe that when a published writer finishes something, she crosses the last *t*, pushes back from the desk, yawns, stretches, and smiles. I do not know anyone who has ever done this, not even once. What happens instead is that you've gone over and over something so many times, and you've weeded and pruned and rewritten, and the person who reads your work for you has given you great suggestions that you have mostly taken— and then finally something inside you just says it's time to get on to the next thing. Of course, there will always be more you could do, but you have to remind yourself that perfectionism is the voice of the oppressor.

There's an image I've heard people in recovery use—that getting all of one's addictions under control is a little like putting an octopus to bed. I think this perfectly describes the process of solving various problems in your final draft. You get a bunch of the octopus's arms neatly tucked under the covers—that is, you've come up with a plot, resolved the conflict between the two main characters, gotten the tone down pat—but two arms are still flailing around. Maybe the dialogue in the first half and the second half don't match, or there is that one character who still seems one-dimensional. But you finally get those arms under the sheets, too, and are about to turn off the lights when another long sucking arm breaks free.

This will probably happen while you are sitting at your desk, kneading your face, feeling burned out and rubberized. Then, even though all the sucking disks on that one tentacle are puckering open and closed, and the slit-shaped pupils of the octopus are looking derisively at you, as if it might suck you to death just because it's bored, and even though you know that your manuscript is not perfect and you'd hoped for so much more, but if you also know that there is simply no more steam in the pressure cooker and that it's the very best you can do for now—well? I think this means that you are done.

Part Two

The Writing Frame of Mind

Looking Around

Writing is about learning to pay attention and to communicate what is going on. Now, if you ask me, what's going on is that we're all up to *here* in it, and probably the most important thing is that we not yell at one another. Otherwise we'd all just be barking away like Pekingese: "Ah! Stuck in the shit! And it's *your* fault, *you* did this . . ." Writing involves seeing people suffer and, as Robert Stone once put it, finding some meaning therein. But you can't do that if you're not respectful. If you look at people and just see sloppy clothes or rich clothes, you're going to get them wrong.

The writer is a person who is standing apart, like the cheese in "The Farmer in the Dell" standing there alone but deciding to take a few notes. You're outside, but you can see things up close through your binoculars. Your job is to present clearly your viewpoint, your line of vision. Your job is to see people as they really are, and to do this, you have to know who you

most compassionate possible sense. Then you can
others. It's simple in concept, but not that easy to
do. My Uncle Ben wrote me a letter twenty years ago in which
he said, "Sometimes you run into someone, regardless of age
or sex, whom you know absolutely to be an independently
operating part of the Whole that goes on all the time inside
yourself, and the eye-motes go *click* and you hear the tribal
tones of voice resonate, and there it is—you recognize them."
That is what I'm talking about: you want your readers' eye-
motes to go click! with recognition as they begin to understand
one of your characters, but you probably won't be able to
present a character that recognizable if you do not first have
self-compassion.

It is relatively easy to look tenderly and with recognition
at a child, especially your own child and especially when he
is being cute or funny, even if he is hurting your feelings. And
it's relatively easy to look tenderly at, say, a chipmunk and
even to see it with some clarity, to see that real life is right
there at your feet, or at least right there in that low branch,
to recognize this living breathing animal with its own agenda,
to hear its sharp, high-pitched chirps, and yet not get all caught
up in its cuteness. I don't want to sound too Cosmica Rama
here, but in those moments, you see that you and the chipmunk
are alike, are a part of a whole. I think we would see this
more often if we didn't have our conscious minds. The conscious mind seems to block that feeling of oneness so we can
function efficiently, maneuver in the world a little bit better,
get our taxes done on time. But it's even possible to have this

feeling when you see—really see—a police officer, when you look right at him and you see that he's a living breathing person who like everyone else is suffering like a son of a bitch, and you don't see him with a transparency over him of all the images of violence and chaos and danger that cops represent. You accept him as an equal.

Obviously, it's harder by far to look at yourself with this same sense of compassionate detachment. Practice helps. As with exercise, you may be sore the first few days, but then you will get a little bit better at it every day. I am learning slowly to bring my crazy pinball-machine mind back to this place of friendly detachment toward myself, so I can look out at the world and see all those other things with respect. Try looking at your mind as a wayward puppy that you are trying to paper train. You don't drop-kick a puppy into the neighbor's yard every time it piddles on the floor. You just keep bringing it back to the newspaper. So I keep trying gently to bring my mind back to what is really there to be seen, maybe to be seen and noted with a kind of reverence. Because if I don't learn to do this, I think I'll keep getting things wrong.

I honestly think in order to be a writer, you have to learn to be reverent. If not, why are you writing? Why are you here?

Let's think of reverence as awe, as presence in and openness to the world. The alternative is that we stultify, we shut down. Think of those times when you've read prose or poetry that is presented in such a way that you have a fleeting sense of being *startled* by beauty or insight, by a glimpse into someone's soul. All of a sudden everything seems to fit together or at least to have some meaning for a moment. This is our goal as writers, I think; to help others have this sense of—please forgive me—wonder, of seeing things anew, things that can catch us off guard, that break in on our small, bordered worlds. When this happens, everything feels more spacious. Try walking around with a child who's going, "Wow, wow! Look at that dirty dog! Look at that burned-down house! Look at that red sky!" And the child points and you look, and you see, and you start going, "Wow! Look at that huge crazy hedge! Look at that teeny little baby! Look at the scary dark cloud!" I think this is how we are supposed to be in the world— present and in awe. Taped to the wall above my desk is a wonderful poem by the Persian mystic, Rumi:

> *God's joy moves from unmarked box to unmarked box,*
> *from cell to cell. As rainwater, down into flowerbed.*
> *As roses, up from ground.*
> *Now it looks like a plate of rice and fish,*
> *now a cliff covered with vines,*
> *now a horse being saddled.*
> *It hides within these,*
> *till one day it cracks them open.*

There is ecstasy in paying attention. You can get into a kind of Wordsworthian openness to the world, where you see in everything the essence of holiness, a sign that God is implicit in all of creation. Or maybe you are not predisposed to see the world sacramentally, to see everything as an outward and

visible sign of inward, invisible grace. This does not mean that
you are worthless Philistine scum. Anyone who wants to can
be surprised by the beauty or pain of the natural world, of
the human mind and heart, and can try to capture just that—
the details, the nuance, what is. If you start to look around,
you will start to see. When what we see catches us off guard,
and when we write it as realistically and openly as possible,
it offers hope. You look around and say, Wow, there's that
same mockingbird; there's that woman in the red hat again.
The woman in the red hat is about hope because she's in it
up to her neck, too, yet every day she puts on that crazy red
hat and walks to town. One of these images might show up
dimly in the lower right quadrant of the imaginary Polaroid
you took; you didn't even know at first that it was part of
the landscape, and here it turns out to evoke something so
deep in you that you can't put your finger on it. Here is one
sentence by Gary Snyder:

> *Ripples on the surface of the water—*
> *were silver salmon passing under—different*
> *from the ripples caused by breezes*

Those words, less than twenty of them, make ripples clear
and bright, distinct again. I have a tape of a Tibetan nun singing
a mantra of compassion over and over for an hour, eight words
over and over, and every line feels different, feels cared about,
and experienced as she is singing. You never once have the
sense that she is glancing down at her watch, thinking, "Jesus

Christ, it's only been fifteen minutes." Forty-five minutes later she is still singing each line distinctly, word by word, until the last word is sung.

Mostly things are not that way, that simple and pure, with so much focus given to each syllable of life as life sings itself. But that kind of attention is the prize. To be engrossed by something outside ourselves is a powerful antidote for the rational mind, the mind that so frequently has its head up its own ass—seeing things in such a narrow and darkly narcissistic way that it presents a colo-rectal theology, offering hope to no one.

The Moral
Point of View

If you find that you start a number of stories or pieces that you don't ever bother finishing, that you lose interest or faith in them along the way, it may be that there is nothing at their center about which you care passionately. You need to put yourself at their center, you and what you believe to be true or right. The core, ethical concepts in which you most passionately believe are the language in which you are writing.

These concepts probably feel like givens, like things no one ever had to make up, that have been true through all cultures and for all time. Telling these truths is your job. You have nothing else to tell us. But needless to say, you can't tell them in a sentence or a paragraph; the truth doesn't come out in bumper stickers. There may be a flickering moment of insight in a one-liner, in a sound bite, but everyday meat-and-potato truth is beyond our ability to capture in a few words. Your whole piece is the truth, not just one shining epigrammatic moment in it. There will need to be some kind of unfolding in order to contain it, and there will need to be layers. We are dealing with the ineffable here—we're out there somewhere between the known and the unknown, trying to reel in both for a closer look. This is why it may take a whole book.

I'm not suggesting that you want to be an author who tells a story in order to teach a moral or deliver a message. If you have a message, as Samuel Goldwyn said, send a telegram. But we feel morally certain of some things, sure that we're right, even while we know how often we've been wrong, and we need to communicate these things. For instance, I used to think that paired opposites were a given, that love was the opposite of hate, right the opposite of wrong. But now I think we sometimes buy into these concepts because it is so much easier to embrace absolutes than to suffer reality. I don't think anything is the opposite of love. Reality is unforgivingly complex.

When you start off writing, if you are anything like me, you may want to fill the page with witticisms and shimmering insights so that the world will see how uniquely smart and sensitive you are. Over the course of time, as you get the knack of doing some writing every day, what seems to happen almost organically is that you end up wanting your characters to act out the drama of humankind. Much of this drama does not involve witticisms and shimmer. Yet this drama is best couched in moral terms; the purpose of most great writing seems to be to reveal in an ethical light who we are. My favorite moment in Jeanne Moreau's latest movie—a comedy called *The Summer House*—takes place in a kitchen, when she proclaims that every human has something to cry about. When mocked by the owner of the kitchen and pressed to say what it is that we have to cry about, she tosses back her head of flaming red hair and says, "The winds of solitude roaring at the edge of infinity." How do we, as individuals and communities, behave with that wind blowing behind us? Are we well behaved, striving for dignity and compassion, or is it every man for himself?

As we live, we begin to discover what helps in life and what hurts, and our characters act this out dramatically. This is moral material. The word *moral* has such bad associations: with fundamentalism, stiff-necked preachers, priggishness. We have to get past that. If your deepest beliefs drive your writing, they will not only keep your work from being contrived but will help you discover what drives your characters. You may find some really good people beneath the packaging and posing—people whom we, your readers, will like, whose company we will rejoice in. We like certain characters because they are good or decent—they internalize some decency in the world that makes them able to take a risk or make a sacrifice for someone else. They let us see that there is in fact some sort of moral compass still at work here, and that we, too, could travel by this compass if we so choose.

In good fiction, we have one eye on the hero or the good guys and a fascinated eye on the bad guys, who may be a lot more interesting. The plot leads all of these people (and us) into dark woods where we find, against all odds, a woman or a man with the compass, and it still points true north. That's the miracle, and it's astonishing. This shaft of light, sometimes only a glimmer, both defines and thwarts the darkness.

Think of a medieval morality play as the model. We love to hear that goodness will triumph over evil, that the fragile prize—humanity, life—will be saved. In formula fiction, evil wins out until the very end, and then against all odds goodness prevails and the hero gets to kiss the girl with the big bosoms. Life is somewhat more complicated than it was in the Middle Ages, but in many ways it is so much the same—violent, terrifying, full of chaos and plague, murderers and thieves. So the acknowledgment that in the midst of ourselves there is still a good part that hasn't been corrupted and destroyed, that we can tap into and reclaim, is most reassuring. When a more or less ordinary character, someone who is both kind and self-serving, somehow finds that place within where he or she is still capable of courage and goodness, we get to see something true that we long for. This is what helps us connect with your characters and with your book. This is what makes it a book we will foist on our friends, a book we will remember, that will accompany us through life.

But you have to believe in your position, or nothing will be driving your work. If you don't believe in what you are saying, there is no point in your saying it. You might as well call it a day and go bowling. However, if you do care deeply about something—if, for instance, you are conservative in the great sense of the word, if you are someone who is trying to

conserve the landscape and the natural world—then this belief
will keep you going as you struggle to get your work done.

To be a good writer, you not only have to write a great
deal but you have to care. You do not have to have a complicated moral philosophy. But a writer always tries, I think,
to be a part of the solution, to understand a little about life
and to pass this on. Even someone as grim and unsentimental
as Samuel Beckett, with his lunatics in garbage cans or up to
their necks in sand, whose lives consist of pawing through the
contents of their purses, stopping to marvel at each item, gives
us great insight into what is true, into what helps. He gets it
right—that we're born astride the grave and that this planet
can feel as cold and uninhabitable as the moon—and he knows
how to make it funny. He smiles an oblique and private smile
at us, the most delicious smile of all, and this changes how
we look at life. A few small things seem suddenly clear, things
to which we can cling, and this makes us feel like part of the
solution. (But perhaps we have the same problem with the
word *solution* as we do with the word *moral*. It sounds so
fixative, and maybe we have gone beyond fixing. Maybe all we
can do is to make our remaining time here full of gentleness
and good humor.)

Or look at the fourteenth Dalai Lama, who is, for my money,
the sanest person currently on earth. He says simply, "My true
religion is kindness." That is a great moral position—practicing
kindness, keeping one's heart open in the presence of suffering.
Unfortunately it does not make great literature. You will need
to embroider it a little. Otherwise you will have a one-sentence

book, and potential agents will look at you as if—as the Texans say—you are perhaps not the brightest porch light on the block.

So a moral position is not a message. A moral position is a passionate caring inside you. We are all in danger now and have a new everything to face, and there is no point gathering an audience and demanding its attention unless you have something to say that is important and constructive. My friend Carpenter says we no longer need Chicken Little to tell us the sky is falling, because it already has. The issue now is how to take care of one another. Some of us are interested in any light you might be able to shed on this, and we will pay a great deal extra if you can make us laugh about it. For some of us, good books and beautiful writing are the ultimate solace, even more comforting than exquisite food. So write about the things that are most important to you. Love and death and sex and survival are important to most of us. Some of us are also interested in God and ecology.

Maybe what you care most passionately about are fasting and high colonics—cappuccino enemas, say. This is fine, but we do not want you to write about them; we will secretly believe that you are simply spiritualizing your hysteria. There are millions of people already doing this at churches and New Age festivals across the land.

Write instead about freedom, freedoms worth fighting for. Human rights begin with and extend to your characters, no matter how horrible they are. You have to respect the qualities that make them who they are. A moral position is not a slogan, or wishful thinking. It doesn't come from outside or above. It begins inside the heart of a character and grows from there. Tell the truth and write about freedom and fight for it, however you can, and you will be richly rewarded. As Molly Ivins put it, freedom fighters don't always win, but they are always right.

Broccoli

There's an old Mel Brooks routine, on the flip side of the "2,000-Year-Old Man," where the psychiatrist tells his patient, "Listen to your broccoli, and your broccoli will tell you how to eat it." And when I first tell my students this, they look at me as if things have clearly begun to deteriorate. But it is as important a concept in writing as it is in real life.

It means, of course, that when you don't know what to do, when you don't know whether your character would do this or that, you get quiet and try to hear that still small voice inside. It will tell you what to do. The problem is that so many of us lost access to our broccoli when we were children. When we listened to our intuition when we were small and then told the grown-ups what we believed to be true, we were often either corrected, ridiculed, or punished. God forbid you should have your own opinions or perceptions—better to have head lice. If you asked innocently, "Why is Mom in the bathroom crying?," you might be told, "Mom isn't crying; Mom has allergies." Or if you said, "Why didn't Dad come home last night?," you might be told brightly, "Dad did come home last night, but then he left again very early." And you nodded, even though you knew that these were lies, because it was important to stay on the adults' good side. There was no one else to take care of you, and if you questioned them too adamantly, you'd probably get sent to your room without dinner, or they'd drive a stake through your ankles and leave you on the hillside above the Mobil station. So you may have gotten into the habit of doubting the voice that was telling you quite clearly what was really going on. It is essential that you get it back.

You need your broccoli in order to write well. Otherwise you're going to sit down in the morning and have only your rational mind to guide you. Then, if you're having a bad day, you're going to crash and burn within half an hour. You'll give up, and maybe even get up, which is worse because a lot of us know that if we just sit there long enough, in whatever shape, we may end up being surprised. Let's say it's only 9:15; now, if you were to stick it out, the image or situation might come to you that would wedge the door open for a character, after which you would only have to get out of the way. Because then the character could come forward and speak and might say something important; it might even be the thing that is most important to him or her, and your plot might suddenly fall into place. You might see how to take that person from good to bad and then back, or whatever. But instead you quit for the day, and you feel defeated and shaken and hopeless, and tomorrow is going to be even harder to face because today you've given up only fifteen minutes after you sat down to work. Remember the scene in *Cat Ballou* where a very drunk Lee Marvin goes from unconscious to ranting to triumphant to roaring to weeping defeat, and then finally passes out? One of the men watching him says, with real awe, "I never seen a man get through a day so fast." Don't let this be you.

You get your confidence and intuition back by trusting yourself, by being militantly on your own side. You need to trust yourself, especially on a first draft, where amid the anxiety and self-doubt, there should be a real sense of your imagination and your memories walking and woolgathering, tramping the hills, romping all over the place. Trust them. Don't look at your feet to see if you are doing it right. Just dance.

You get your intuition back when you make space for it, when you stop the chattering of the rational mind. The rational mind doesn't nourish you. You assume that it gives you the truth, because the rational mind is the golden calf that this culture worships, but this is not true. Rationality squeezes out much that is rich and juicy and fascinating.

Sometimes intuition needs coaxing, because intuition is a little shy. But if you try not to crowd it, intuition often wafts up from the soul or subconscious, and then becomes a tiny fitful little flame. It will be blown out by too much compulsion and manic attention, but will burn quietly when watched with gentle concentration.

So try to calm down, get quiet, breathe, and listen. Squint at the screen in your head, and if you look, you will see what you are searching for, the details of the story, its direction— maybe not right this minute, but eventually. If you stop trying to control your mind so much, you'll have intuitive hunches about what this or that character is all about. It is hard to stop controlling, but you can do it. If your character suddenly pulls a half-eaten carrot out of her pocket, let her. Later you can ask yourself if this rings true. Train yourself to hear that small inner voice. Most people's intuitions are drowned out by folk sayings. We have a moment of real feeling or insight, and then we come up with a folk saying that captures the insight in a kind of wash. The intuition may be real and ripe, fresh with possibilities, but the folk saying is guaranteed to be a cliché, stale and self-contained.

Take the attitude that what you are thinking and feeling is valuable stuff, and then be naive enough to get it all down on paper. But be careful: if your intuition says that your story sucks, make sure it really is your intuition and not your mother. "I see this character in a purple sharkskin suit," you suddenly think, and then the voice of the worried mother says, "No, no, put him in something respectable." But if you listen to the worried mother, pretty soon you'll be asleep and so will your reader. Your intuition will make it a much wilder and more natural ride; it may show you what would really jump out from behind those trees over there. You won't always get a clear, panting, "Aha! Purple sharkskin suit!" More often you will hear a subterranean murmur. It may sound like one of the many separate voices that make up the sounds of a creek. Or it may come in code, oblique and sneaky, creeping in from around the corner. If you shine too much light on it, it may draw back and fade away.

I think a major step in learning to rely on your intuition is to find a usable metaphor for it. Broccoli is so ridiculous that it works for me. A friend says that his intuition is his animal: "My animal thinks this," he says, or "My animal hates that." But whatever you come up with needs to suggest a voice that you are not trying to control. If you're lost in the forest, let the horse find the way home. *You* have to stop directing, because you will only get in the way.

Writing is about hypnotizing yourself into believing in yourself, getting some work done, then unhypnotizing yourself and going over the material coldly. There will be many mistakes, many things to take out and others that need to be added. You just aren't always going to make the right decision. My friend Terry says that when you need to make a decision, in your work or otherwise, and you don't know what to do, just do one thing or the other, because the worst that can happen is that you will have made a terrible mistake. So let the plot go left in this one place instead of right, or let your character decide to go back to her loathsome passive-aggressive husband. Maybe it was the right thing, maybe not. If not, go back and try something else. Some of us tend to think that what we do and say and decide and write are cosmically important things. But they're not. If you don't know which way to go, keep it simple. Listen to your broccoli. Maybe it will know what to do. Then, if you've worked in good faith for a couple of hours but cannot hear it today, have some lunch.

Radio Station KFKD

I need to bring up radio station KFKD, or K-Fucked, here. It is perhaps the single greatest obstacle to listening to your broccoli that exists for writers. Then I promise I'll never mention it again.

If you are not careful, station KFKD will play in your head twenty-four hours a day, nonstop, in stereo. Out of the right speaker in your inner ear will come the endless stream of self-aggrandizement, the recitation of one's specialness, of how much more open and gifted and brilliant and knowing and misunderstood and humble one is. Out of the left speaker will be the rap songs of self-loathing, the lists of all the things one doesn't do well, of all the mistakes one has made today and over an entire lifetime, the doubt, the assertion that everything that one touches turns to shit, that one doesn't do relationships well, that one is in every way a fraud, incapable of selfless love, that one has no talent or insight, and on and on and on.

You might as well have heavy-metal music piped in through headphones while you're trying to get your work done. You have to get things quiet in your head so you can hear your characters and let them guide your story.

The best way to get quiet, other than the combination of extensive therapy, Prozac, and a lobotomy, is first to notice that the station is on. KFKD is on every single morning when I sit down at my desk. So I sit for a moment and then say a small prayer—please help me get out of the way so I can write what wants to be written. Sometimes ritual quiets the racket. Try it. Any number of things may work for you—an altar, for instance, or votive candles, sage smudges, small-animal sacrifices, especially now that the Supreme Court has legalized them. (I cut out the headline the day this news came out and taped it above the kitty's water dish.) Rituals are a good signal to your unconscious that it is time to kick in.

You might also consider trying to breathe. This is not something that I remember to do very often, and I do not normally like to hang around people who talk about slow conscious breathing; I start to worry that a nice long discussion of aromatherapy is right around the corner. But these slow conscious breathers are on to something, because if you try to follow your breath for a while, it will ground you in relative silence.

So. You sit down to work at nine in the morning, and do the prayer or the small-animal sacrifice or whatever, and then breathe for a moment, and try to focus on where your characters are, only to discover that your mind has begun to wander just a little. Typically, you may find yourself wondering how some really awful writer you know is doing, and why he is doing so much better than you, and what it will be like to be on David Letterman's show, and whether he will mock you or laugh at all your jokes and let you be his new best friend, and what you should eat for lunch, and what it would feel like for your hair to be on fire or for someone—like a critic or something—to stick a sharp object into your eye. Not to worry. Gently bring your mind back to your work.

Let's say your character is sitting with his grown son beneath a cypress tree on a lion-colored hillside, chewing over in the sourest possible voice the few ecstatic moments of his life, and all you are going to do this morning is to squint along with him, and listen, and possibly find out what some of those moments might have been. After a minute, you begin to see your man in someone's grassy backyard, not long ago, playing Ping-Pong with a younger man, a hippie, and they are not competing, just hitting together, and you begin to capture this on paper, and after two sentences you begin to worry about complete financial collapse, what it will be like to live in a car, and then your mother calls joyfully to tell you that something fantastic just happened to someone who was mean to you in the eighth grade. You get off the phone, and your mind has become a frog brain that scientists have saturated with caffeine. You may need another minute to bring it back to the man's moment in that grassy backyard. Close your eyes. Breathe. Begin again.

I'm sorry, I wish that there were a sharper, slicker way to

do this, but this seems to be the only solution. Believe me, I hate natural solutions, or at any rate they are the last ones I turn to. Two nights ago I showed up to teach my class with a raw chest and a raging sore throat, the kind that feels like cancer of the trachea. I happen to have two doctors in this class, and one of them tried to assure me that it probably wasn't tracheal cancer, that in fact the viral cloud of mid-autumn had descended and many people were having similar symptoms. The other doctor recommended drinking really, really hot water. "Hot water?" I said. "Hot *water?* I should be home hooked up to an epidural, drinking codeine cough syrup, and you're prescribing hot water?" Then I threatened to lower his grade. (Of course, this is not a graded workshop, so my students tend to roll their eyes when I threaten them.) At the break, that doctor brought me a cup of boiling water, as though for tea but without the tea bag, and I drank it. My throat and chest stopped aching about twenty seconds later.

I hate that.

Still, breathing calmly can help you get into a position where the workings of your characters' hearts and the things people say on the streets of your story can be heard above the sound of KFKD. When you are in that position, you will know. I am struggling very hard not to use the word *harmony* here. So let me tell you a quick story.

Last summer I got a call from a producer in New York who wanted me to fly east two days later, stay in town over-night, do her TV talk show, and fly home. I thought long and hard about whether I should—for about thirty seconds. Of course I wanted to go. But I would have to make arrangements for Sam to stay overnight with his grandparents, and I needed to catch a return flight that would get me back in time to teach my workshop the next night, and the only one that could do that involved a layover at Dallas–Fort Worth. A layover at Dallas–Fort Worth is something for which, believe me, I am not remotely well enough. So I shared all this with the producer and took off for a committee meeting I had at church.

I was a mess. Out of the right speaker, KFKD was playing a dress rehearsal of the TV talk show and of subsequent appearances with Dave and Arsenio. Out of the left speaker was a call-in program on airplane crashes, with descriptions of what happens to the body on impact.

I got to church and my committee had not yet assembled, but four of the church's elders—all women—three African Americans and one white, were having a prayer meeting. They were praying for homeless children. "Can we discuss my personal problems for a moment?" I asked.

They nodded and I told them all about my airline fears and how many moving parts there were to this trip east. They nodded again. They seemed to believe that between Jesus and a travel agent, things could probably be worked out. I sighed. My meeting was starting in another room, so I trudged off. My mind spun with images of the talk show, the airplane crash, and the madman with the Uzi at Dallas–Fort Worth. I was having a little trouble concentrating. The meeting ended, and on my way out, a little book on prayer caught my eye. I picked it up and stuck it in my purse, figuring I could look at it over dinner and then return it the next Sunday.

All the way to the hamburger joint, I worried that I would be involved in a car accident and the book would be found on me. My survivors would know I had finally snapped, that I had become one of those fundamentalists who think the world is going to end tomorrow right after lunch. I made it to the restaurant, though, and when I sat down, I took out the little book. I opened it before I got it out of my purse so the cover wouldn't show, as if it were the rankest sort of pornography, like *Big Beautiful Butts* or something. I started to read and within a page came upon this beautiful passage: "The Gulf Stream will flow through a straw provided the straw is aligned to the Gulf Stream, and not at cross purposes with it."

To make a long story short, I flew to New York and everything went fine. I didn't have to stop in Dallas–Fort Worth, and I got home in time to teach my class. So now I always tell my students about the Gulf Stream: that what it means for us, for writers, is that we need to align ourselves with the river of the story, the river of the unconscious, of memory and sensibility, of our characters' lives, which can then pour through us, the straw. When KFKD is playing, we are at cross purposes with the river. So we need to sit there, and breathe, calm ourselves down, push back our sleeves, and begin again.

Jealousy

Of all the voices you'll hear on KFKD, the most difficult to subdue may be that of jealousy. Jealousy is such a direct attack on whatever measure of confidence you've been able to muster. But if you continue to write, you are probably going to have to deal with it, because some wonderful, dazzling successes are going to happen for some of the most awful, angry, undeserving writers you know—people who are, in other words, not you.

This is going to happen because the public herd mentality is not swayed by the magic that happens when mind and heart and muse and hand and paper work together. Rather, it is guided by talk shows and movie producers and TV commercials. Still, you'd probably like the caribou herd to run in your direction for a while. Most of us secretly want this. But maybe the herd is going to stuff itself on lichen and then waddle after some really undeserving writers instead. Those writers will get the place on the best-seller list, the movie sales, the huge advances, and the nice big glossy pictures in the national magazines where the photo editors have airbrushed out the excessively long eyeteeth, the wrinkles, and the horns. The writer you most admire in the world will give them rave reviews in the *Times* or blurbs for the paperback edition. They will buy houses, big houses, or second houses that are actually as nice, or nicer, than the first ones. And you are going to want to throw yourself down the back stairs, especially if the person is a friend.

You are going to feel awful beyond words. You are going to have a number of days in a row where you hate everyone and don't believe in anything. If you do know the author whose turn it is, he or she will inevitably say that it will be your turn next, which is what the bride always says to you at each successive wedding, while you grow older and more decayed. It can wreak just the tiniest bit of havoc with your self-esteem to find that you are hoping for small bad things to happen to this friend—for, say, her head to blow up. Or for him to wake up one morning with a pain in his prostate, because I don't care how rich and successful someone is, if you wake up having to call your doctor and ask for a finger massage, it's going to be a long day. You get all caught up in such fantasies because you feel, once again, like the kid outside the candy-store window, and you believe that this friend, this friend whom you now hate, has all the candy. You believe that success is bringing this friend inordinate joy and serenity and security and that her days are easier. She's going to live to be one hundred and twenty, he's never going to die—the people who are going to die are the good people, like you. But this is not true. Money won't guarantee these writers much of anything, except that now they have a much more expensive set of problems. The pressure on their lives has actually intensified.

Good, fine, you think. I'm into intensity; those are the problems I want.

But do you really?

Yes. I really do.

But some of the loneliest, most miserable, neurotic, despicable people we know have been the most successful in the world.

Right—but it would be different for me. I would not fall for my own press clippings. I would not mention my achievements all the time. I would not say things like "Boy, you think it's raining hard today? I remember one day—I think it was the year I got the Guggenheim—it *really* rained hard." You'd never do that, unlike other people you could mention.

That's very nice. It's all going to happen to somebody else anyway. Bank on it. Jealousy is one of the occupational hazards of being a writer, and the most degrading. And I, who have been the Leona Helmsley of jealousy, have come to believe that the only things that help ease or transform it are (a) getting older, (b) talking about it until the fever breaks, and (c) using it as material. Also, someone somewhere along the line is going to be able to make you start laughing about it, and then you will be on your way home.

I went through a very bad bout of jealousy last year, when someone with whom I am (or rather was) friendly did extremely well. It felt like every few days she'd have more good news about how well her book was doing, until it seemed that she was going to be set for life. It threw me for a loop. I am a better writer than she is. A lot of my writer friends do very well, hugely well, and I'm not jealous of them. I do not know why that is, but it's true. But when it happened for her, I would sit listening to her discuss her latest successes over the phone, praying that I could get off the line before I started barking. I was literally oozing unhappiness, like a sump.

My deepest belief is that to live as if we're dying can set us free. Dying people teach you to pay attention and to forgive and not to sweat the small things. So every time this friend called, I tried to will myself into forgiving both of us. I had been around someone from the South that summer who was always exclaiming, "Isn't that great?"—only she made it almost rhyme with "bright." So when my friend would call with her lastest good news, always presented humbly like some born-again-Christian Miss America contestant, I'd say, "Isn't that gright, huh? Isn't that gright?"

She would say, "You are so supportive. Some of my other friends are having trouble with this."

I'd say, "How could I not be supportive? It's just so darn gright."

But I always wanted to ask, "Could I have the names and numbers of some of your other friends?"

Sometimes I would get off the phone and cry.

After a while I started asking people for help.

One person reminded me of what Jean Rhys once wrote, that all of us writers are little rivers running into one lake, that what is good for one is good for all, that we all collectively share in one another's success and acclaim. I said, "You are a very, very angry person."

My therapist said that jealousy is a secondary emotion, that it is born out of feeling excluded and deprived, and that if I worked on those age-old feelings, I would probably break through the jealousy. I tried to get her to give me a prescription for Prozac, but she said that this other writer was in my life to help me heal my past. She said this writer had helped bring up a lifetime's worth of feeling that other families were happier than ours, that other families had some owner's manual to go by. She said it was once again that business of comparing my insides to other people's outsides. She said to go ahead and feel the feelings. I did. They felt like shit.

My friend, the writer I was so jealous of, would call and say, like some Southern belle, "I just don't know why God is giving me so much money this year." And I would do my Lamaze for a moment, and say, "Isn't that gright?" I have never felt like such a loser in my life.

I called a very wise writer I know who's been in Alcoholics Anonymous for years, who spends half his time helping others get sober. I asked him what he would tell a newcomer who was in the throes of insanity or, say hypothetically, jealousy.

"I just listen," he said. "They all tell me these incredibly long, self-important, convoluted stories. And then I say one of three things: I say, 'Uh-huh,' I say, 'Hmmm,' I say, 'Too bad.' " I laughed. Then I started telling him about this awful friend I had who was doing so well. He was silent for a moment. Then he said, "Uh-huh."

Next I talked to my slightly overweight alcoholic gay Catholic priest friend. I said, "Do you get jealous?"

He said, "When I see a man my own age in great shape, and I feel all conflicted, wishing I were that thin and yet at the same time wanting to lick him, is that jealousy or is that appreciation?"

It was hard to get anyone to say anything that would make the jealousy go away or change into something else. I felt like the wicked stepsister in a fairy tale. I told another friend, and she read me some lines by a Lakota Sioux: "Sometimes I go about pitying myself. And all the while I am being carried on great winds across the sky." That is so beautiful, I said; and I am so mentally ill.

Those lines, however, offered the beginning of a solution. They made the first tiny crack in my prison wall. I was waiting for the kind of solution where God reaches down and touches you with his magic wand and all of a sudden I would be fixed, like a broken toaster oven. But this was not the way it happened. Instead, I got one angstrom unit better, day by day.

Another piece of the solution came when a poem by Clive James, called "The Book of My Enemy Has Been Remaindered," appeared one Sunday in *The New York Times Book Review.* "The book of my enemy has been remaindered," it begins, "And I am pleased." It helped more than words can say. Oh, what blessed relief for someone to be as jealous and spiteful as me and to make those feelings funny. I called everyone whose advice I had sought and read it to them. Everybody howled with recognition.

Yet another piece of the solution dropped into place when my friend Judy said that the problem was trying to *stop* the jealousy and competitiveness, and that the main thing was not to let it fuel my self-loathing. She said it was nuts for me to try to be happy for this other writer. I cannot tell you how much this helped. I was raised in a culture that promotes this competitiveness, this insatiability, this fantasy of needing hundreds of thousands of dollars a year, and then, in the next breath, shames you for any feelings of longing or envy or fear that it will always be someone else's turn. I was only doing what I had been groomed to do.

So I started getting my sense of humor back. I started telling myself that if you want to know how God feels about money, look at whom she gives it to. This cheered me up no end, even though my closest friends have lots of money. I told myself that historically when people do too well too quickly, they are a Greek tragedy waiting to happen. I, who did not do too well too quickly and who was in fact not doing too well over time, was actually in the catbird seat. I was not going to end up the cocky heroine in an ugly hubris drama. This is not to be underestimated. My nerves are shot as it is; the last thing I need would be an onslaught of thunder and silent screams, with cymbals, fangs, winds pushing forest fires across the land; I mean, who *needs* it?

Then I started to write about my envy. I got to look in some cold dark corners, see what was there, shine a little light on what we all have in common. Sometimes this human stuff is slimy and pathetic—jealousy especially so—but better to feel it and talk about it and walk through it than to spend a lifetime being silently poisoned.

Now I felt like I was getting somewhere, after all those weeks of emotionally swimming the English Channel, cold and afraid. Then I saw a documentary on TV about a couple with AIDS. And all the pieces of the solution finally came together.

There was a lot of footage in that movie of ravaged bodies, the sorts of bodies we usually recoil from. One of the men in the couple had an emaciated back entirely purple with Kaposi's. But once you, the viewer, got to know the spirit inside, you could see the beauty of that sick person lying under the mounds of quilts that friends had made. You could see the amazing fortitude of people going through horror with grace, looking right into the pit and seeing that this is what you've got, this disease, or maybe even this jealousy. So you do as well as you can with it. And this ravaged body or wounded psyche can and should still be cared for as softly and tenderly as possible.

The more I wrote about it and the more I thought of the movie, the angrier I got at how often this writer friend mentioned her money to me, because that summer Sam and I had almost none, and she knew this. I kept writing about my childhood, about how often I had longed for what other girls had and for what other families seemed to be about. I taped

Hillel's line to the wall by my desk: "I get up. I walk. I fall down. Meanwhile, I keep dancing." The way I dance is by writing. So I wrote about trying to pay closer attention to the world, about taking things less seriously, moving more slowly, stepping outside more often. Eventually what I was writing got funnier and compassion broke through, for me and also for my writer friend. And at this point I told her, as kindly as possible, that I needed a sabbatical from our friendship. Life really is so short. And finally I felt that my jealousy and I were strangely beautiful, like the men in the AIDS movie, doing the dance of the transformed self, dancing like an old long-legged bird.

Part Three

Help Along the Way

Index Cards

I like to think that Henry James said his classic line, "A writer is someone on whom nothing is lost," while looking for his glasses, and that they were on top of his head. We have so much to remember these days. So we make all these lists, filled with hope that they will remind us of all the important things to do and buy and mail, all the important calls we need to make, all the ideas we have for short stories or articles. And yet by the time you get around to everything on any one list, you're already behind on another. Still, I believe in lists and I believe in taking notes, and I believe in index cards for doing both.

I have index cards and pens all over the house—by the bed, in the bathroom, in the kitchen, by the phones, and I have them in the glove compartment of my car. I carry one with me in my back pocket when I take my dog for a walk. In fact, I carry it folded lengthwise, if you need to know, so that, God forbid, I won't look bulky. You may want to consider doing the same. I don't even know you, but I bet you have enough on your mind without having to worry about whether or not you look bulky. So whenever I am leaving the house without my purse—in which there are actual notepads, let alone index cards—I fold an index card lengthwise in half, stick it in my back pocket along with a pen, and head out, knowing that if I have an idea, or see something lovely or strange or for any reason worth remembering, I will be able to jot down a couple of words to remind me of it. Sometimes, if I overhear or think of an exact line of dialogue or a transition, I write it down verbatim. I stick the card back in my pocket. I might be walking along the salt marsh, or out at Phoenix Lake, or in the express line at Safeway, and suddenly I hear something wonderful that makes me want to smile or snap my fingers—as if it has just come back to me—and I take out my index card and scribble it down.

I have an index card beside me right now on which I scribbled, "Pammy, Demi Moore." Those words capture an entire movie for me, of one particular day last year, six months before Pammy died.

We were outside in her garden. The sky was blue and cloudless, everything was in bloom, and she wore a little lavender cotton cap. She was doing very well that day, except that she was dying. (My father's oncologist once assured him, "You're a very, very healthy fifty-five-year-old man, except, of course, for the brain cancer.") We were lying on chaise longues, in T-shirts and shorts, eating miniature Halloween chocolate bars. Sam was pulling Pammy's two-year-old daughter Rebecca around the garden in a little red wagon.

"I'm a little depressed," Pammy said. One day not long before, she had said that all she had to do to get really, really depressed was to think of Rebecca, and all she had to do to get really, really *joyful* was to think of Rebecca. "I'm actually quite depressed," she said.

"I don't see why."

"What's the silver lining here? I can't seem to remember today."

"The silver lining is that you're not going to have to see any more naked pregnant pictures of Demi Moore."

She looked at me for a moment with real wonder. "God," she said, "that's a lot—I hadn't even thought of that." And she was very funny again for the rest of the day, happy to be with the children and me.

It was such a rare scene that you would think I would remember it forever. I used to think that if something was important enough, I'd remember it until I got home, where I could simply write it down in my notebook like some normal functioning member of society.

But then I wouldn't.

I'd get home, remembering that I had thought of or heard the perfect image or lines to get my characters from the party in the old house on the hill to their first day on the new job, or to their childhood playhouse, or wherever it was that they seemed to think they were supposed to be next. And I'd stand there trying to see it, the way you try to remember a dream, where you squint and it's right there on the tip of your psychic tongue but you can't get it back. The image is gone. That is one of the worst feelings I can think of, to have had a wonderful moment or insight or vision or phrase, to know you had it, and then to lose it. So now I use index cards.

One of the things that happens when you give yourself permission to start writing is that you start thinking like a writer. You start seeing everything as material. Sometimes you'll sit down or go walking and your thoughts will be on one aspect of your work, or one idea you have for a small scene, or a general portrait of one of the characters you are working with, or you'll just be completely blocked and hopeless and wondering why you shouldn't just go into the kitchen and have a nice glass of warm gin straight out of the cat dish. And then, unbidden, seemingly out of nowhere, a thought or image arrives. Some will float into your head like goldfish, lovely, bright orange, and weightless, and you follow them like a child looking at an aquarium that was thought to be without fish. Others will step out of the shadows like Boo Radley and make you catch your breath or take a step backward. They're often so rich, these unbidden thoughts, and so clear that they feel indelible. But I say write them all down anyway.

Now, I have a number of writer friends who do not take notes out there in the world, who say it's like not taking notes in class but *listening* instead. I think that if you have the kind of mind that retains important and creative thoughts—that is, if your mind still works—you're very lucky and you should not be surprised if the rest of us do not want to be around you. I actually have one writer friend——whom I think I will probably be getting rid of soon——who said to me recently that if you don't remember it when you get home, it probably wasn't that important. And I felt eight years old again, with something important to say that had suddenly hopped down one of the rabbit holes in my mind, while an adult nearby was saying priggishly, "Well! It must not have been very important then."

So you have to decide how you feel about this. You may have a perfectly good memory and be able to remember three hours later what you came up with while walking on the mountain or waiting at the dentist's. And then again, you may not. If it feels natural, if it helps you to remember, take notes. It's not cheating. It doesn't say anything about your character. If your mind is perhaps the merest bit disorganized, it probably just means that you've lost a little ground. It may be all those drugs you took when you were younger, all that nonhabit-forming marijuana that you smoked on a daily basis for twenty years. It may be that you've had children. When a child comes out of your body, it arrives with about a fifth of your brain clutched in its little hand, like those babies born clutching IUDs. So for any number of reasons, it's only fair to let yourself take notes.

My index-card life is not efficient or well organized. Hostile, aggressive students insist on asking what I *do* with all my index cards. And all I can say is that I have them, I took notes on them, and the act of having written something down gives me a fifty-fifty shot at having it filed away now in my memory. If I'm working on a book or an article, and I've taken some notes on index cards, I keep them with that material, paperclip them to a page of rough draft where that idea or image might bring things to life. Or I stack them on my desk along with the pages for the particular chapter or article I'm working on, so I can look at them. When I get stuck or lost or the jungle drums start beating in my head, proclaiming that the jig is about to be up and I don't know what I'm doing and the well has run dry, I'll look through my index cards. I try to see if there's a short assignment on any of them that will get me writing again, give me a small sense of confidence, help me put down one damn word after another, which is, let's face it, what writing finally boils down to.

There are index cards on my desk that record things I thought of or saw or remembered or overheard in the last week or so. There are index cards from a couple of years ago. There is even one index card from six or seven years ago, when I was walking along the salt marsh between Sausalito and Mill Valley. Bicyclists were passing me on both sides, and I wasn't paying much attention until suddenly a woman rode past wearing some sort of lemon perfume. And in a split second I was in one of those Proustian olfactory flashbacks, twenty-five or so years before, in the kitchen of one of my aunts, with her many children, my cousins, on a hot summer's day. I was the eldest, at eight or so, and my aunt and uncle had just gotten divorced. She was sad and worried, and I think to soothe herself and help her wounded ego, she had done a little retail therapy: she'd gone to the store and spent several dollars on a lemonade-making contraption.

Of course, it goes without saying that to make lemonade, all you need is a pitcher, a lemon-juice squeezer, ice cubes, water, lemons, and sugar. That's all. Oh, and a long spoon. But my aunt was a little depressed, and this lemonade-making thing must have seemed like something that would be fun and would maybe hydrate her life a little, filling her desiccated spirit with nice, cool, sweet lemonade. The contraption consisted of a glass pitcher, with a lemon squeezer that fit on top and that had a holding tank for the lemon juice. What you did was to fill the pitcher with water and ice cubes and sugar, then put the squeezer—with its holding tank—on top, squeeze a bunch of lemons, then pour the lemon juice from the holding tank into the pitcher. Finally, you got your long spoon and stirred. The lemon googe and seeds stayed on top in the juice squeezer. The whole thing was very efficient, but if you thought about it too long, totally stupid, too.

So there we were in the kitchen, the five cousins and me, crowded around her at the sink as she proudly made us lemonade. She put the cold water in the pitcher, added ice cubes, lots of sugar, put the juicer lid on top, squeezed a dozen lemons, and then began to take glasses down from the cupboards. Wait! we older ones wanted to cry out, you haven't poured in the lemon juice. Stop! Mistakes are being made! But she got out jelly glasses, plastic glasses, a couple of brilliant aluminum glasses, and poured seven servings. There we were, six anxious black-belt codependents, unable to breathe, with a longing for everything to be Okay and for her not to feel sad anymore. She raised her glass to us as a toast, and we all took sips of our sugary ice water, and my aunt's hands were so lemony from cutting and squeezing all those lemons that she must have tasted lemon. We all stared at her helplessly as we drank our sugar water, then smiled and raised our glasses like we were doing a soft-drink commercial, and held them out for more.

I perfectly remembered, there on the salt marsh, the crummy linoleum on my aunt's kitchen floor, graying beige speckled with black, and how it wore away to all black near the sink, and how at its most worn place, rotten wood showed through. And how all those cousins, some so young they must have thought ice-cold sugar water was about as good as the getting got, stood at the sink with us older kids, in a ring around my aunt. And how close I felt to them all, how much a part of the wheel.

It touches me so deeply, the poignancy of the crummy linoleum, of my aunt's pain and her pride in her lemonade-making machine, of all the ways in which we try to comfort ourselves, of her wanting to make us better lemonade, of us wanting to make her better, the enthusiasm with which we drank and held out our glasses, as if we were hoisting steins at Oktoberfest. And I hadn't remembered any of this in twenty-five years.

Now, maybe I'm not going to use it anywhere. All the index card says is "The lemonade-making thing." But it's like a snippet from a movie, a vignette of a family in pain, managing to survive, one of those rare moments when people's hearts are opened by disappointment and love, and for just a few minutes, against all odds, everything is more or less Okay.

Sometimes I'll be driving along, and all of a sudden words form in my mind that solve some technical problem for me. I may have been trying all morning long to show that time has been passing for my characters, without resorting to old-movie techniques where leaves of a calendar blow out the window or the hands of a clock spin. These techniques do not translate well to the written word. It's a wonderful feeling when you're reading something by someone else, and the writer has aged exactly the right detail so that you know the story is picking up again sometime later. Sometimes the seasons change, or children start school, or beards grow long, or pets go gray. But sometimes in your own writing you can't find the way to make time pass invisibly, and you will not be aided in this by sitting at your desk staring bitterly at your words, trying to will it to happen. Instead, all of a sudden when you're wrestling with the dog or paying the electric bill, you might look up and know that something is coming to you that might really matter, only you can't quite reel it in. It's like watching someone on a ventilator rise again and again to the surface, like a trapped fish, and you stay with the person, and sometimes he or she blinks awake. And so, if you hold some space open, an image may come to you. Then, for goodness sakes, jot it down.

I have an index card here on which is written, "Six years

later, the memory of the raw fish cubes continued to haunt her," which I thought might make a great transitional line. But I have so far not found a place for it. You are welcome to use it if you can.

I eventually throw away a lot of my index cards, either because I use what's on them in a paragraph somewhere or because it turns out that the thought wasn't all that interesting. Many index cards on which I write in the middle of the night tend to be incoherent, like some incredibly bright math major thinking about oranges or truth while on LSD. Some contain great quotes that I share with my students, although I unfortunately often forget to write down whose quote it is. Like this one, for instance: "What lies behind us and what lies before us are tiny matters, compared to what lies within us." Now, I'm almost positive Ralph Waldo Emerson said this, but with my luck some critic will point out that it was really Georgette Mosbacher. (Who was it that said, "A critic is someone who comes onto the battlefield after the battle is over and shoots the wounded"? I have it written on an index card somewhere. . . .) Other cards just sort of live with me, in little piles and drifts. My son will probably have to deal with them someday, after my death. They are my equivalent of all the cats that those nutty Bouvier aunts own. But my cards do not smell or shed or go wee-wee on the floors, and I think Sam should be aware that he is getting off easy. Most of them will not make much sense to him. There are many with just one or two words on them that would have reminded me of entire scenes and empires, but he will have to stand there scratching his head.

But he will also find some dated in the early nineties, and they will contain complete stories about how he blew me away, how he made me shake my head with wonder and a kind of relief. Like this one, dated 9-17-93:

> *Sam and I walked Bill and Adair up to their car after dinner. Crisp cold starry night. Bill, holding Sam, inhaled deeply. "Doesn't it smell wonderful, Sam?" he said. Sam inhaled deeply, too, like he was smelling a delicious meal, looked off into space, and said, "It smells like moon."*

Now that memory won't be lost. I'm not sure if I will use it in my writing—actually, I guess I just did—but I know it won't be lost.

Nor will the details of an early morning the two of us spent recently in an emergency room, where Sam was having his first asthma attack. We were both afraid and sad and did not quite know what was going on, but Sam was hooked up to a nebulizer, with a mask over his mouth and nose, and I was sitting beside him on his bed, wishing I had thought to grab a toy as we left the house. So I looked inside my purse and managed to come up with a tiny box of crayons from a restaurant and two used index cards. One contained a shopping list, the other a brief description of the sky.

I drew a terrible giant on the blank side of each card. Sam, sucking away at his mask, watched me with fear. Next I poked holes in each of the giants' right hands, and stuck tongue depressors through the holes. Then I staged a vigorous, clicking sword fight. Sam's eyes grew wide, and he smiled. After a long while he could breathe again freely, and we were told we could go home. But before we did, I dismantled the giants, stuck the card with the shopping list in my back pocket and, on the back of the other, scribbled down this story.

Calling Around

There are an enormous number of people out there with invaluable information to share with you, and all you have to do is pick up the phone. They love it when you do, just as you love it when people ask if they can pick your brain about something you happen to know a great deal about—or, as in my case, have a number of impassioned opinions on. Say you happen to know a lot about knots, or penguins, or cheeses, and the right person asks you to tell him or her everything you know. What a wonderful and rare experience. Usually what happens in real life is that people ask you questions you can't remember the answer to, like what you came into the kitchen to get, or what happened on the Fourth of July in 1776, and you sit there thinking, "God, I knew that; it's right there on the tip of my tongue, let's see—Okay, wait, the Constitution? No, wait, shit, I used to know..." When you do actually know a bit about something, it is such a pleasure to be asked a lot of questions about it.

This is one great reason to call around. Another is that if you make the phone call while sitting at your computer, you can consider it part of that day's work. It's not shirking. Being a writer guarantees that you will spend too much time alone—and that as a result, your mind will begin to warp. If you are in a small workspace, your brain will begin breathing and contracting like the sets in *Dr. Caligari*. You may begin showing signs of schizophrenia—like you'll stare at the word *schizophrenia* so long that it will start to look wrong and you won't be able to find it in the dictionary and you'll start to think you made it up, and then you'll notice a tiny mouth sore, one of those tiny canker sores that your tongue can't keep away from, that feels like a wound the size of a marble, but when you go to study it in the mirror, you see that it is a white spot roughly as big as a pinhead. Still, the next thing you know—because you are spending *too much time alone*—you are convinced that you have mouth cancer, just like good old Sigmund, and you know instantly that doctors will have to cut away half of your jaw, trying to save your miserable obsessive-compulsive head from being cannibalized by the cancer, and you'll have to go around wearing a hood over your entire face, and no one will ever want to kiss you again, not that they ever really did.

I don't think there is anything wrong with this way of thinking, only that it is ultimately not all that productive. So you might as well try to get something done. And it's better if contact with another human being is involved. One thing I know for sure about raising children is that every single day a kid needs discipline—so it's useful to give yourself a minimum quota of three hundred words a day. But also every single day a kid needs a break. So think of calling around as giving yourself a break.

The truth is that there are simply going to be times when you can't go forward in your work until you find out something about the place you grew up, when it was still a railroad town, or what the early stages of shingles are like, or what your character would actually experience the first week of beauty school. So figure out who would have this information and give that person a call. It's best if you can think of someone who's witty and articulate, so you can steal all of his or her material. Also, of course, it's just more interesting to be on the phone with someone who's sort of keen. But these qualities are not absolutely necessary, because you may just be looking for one piece of information, or even just one word, and you do not need a whole lot of background or humor to go with it. And it may also turn out that in searching for this one bit of information, something else will turn up that you absolutely could not have known would be out there waiting for you.

For instance, when I was writing my second novel, I got to the part where the man comes over for his first date with the woman and brings with him a bottle of champagne. He removes the foil. We get to see his hands, which are beautiful, long and broad with white moons on his big square fingernails, so lovely that they almost make up for the fact that he is

147

wearing a yellow polyester shirt. Also, it is in his favor that he has brought along a nice bottle of champagne; the woman loves to drink. So the man has peeled the foil away, and then begins to untwist and remove that wire thing that covers all champagne corks.

Now, I've always thought of that wire thing—that little helmet—as the wire thing, and that is how everyone I've ever known refers to it: "Honey, will you take the wire thing off the champagne? I just had my nails done." "Oh, look, Skippy's playing with that little wire thing; I hope she doesn't cut her little lips on it . . ."

But it must have a name, right? I mean, boxes of them don't just arrive at wineries—five-hundred-count Wire Things. They have to have a label. So I called the Christian Brothers Winery, whose vineyard is near the Russian River. I got a busy signal. I really did. So I sat there staring off into space. I watched the movie in my mind of the many times I'd passed those vineyards and remembered how, especially in the early fall, a vineyard is about as voluptuous a place as you can find on earth: the sense of lushness and abundance; the fullness of the clumps of grapes that hang, mammarian, and give off an ancient autumnal smell, semiprotected from the sun by their leaves. The grapes are so incredibly beautiful that you can't help but be thrilled. If you aren't—if you only see someone's profit or that in another month there will be rotten fruit all over the ground—someone has gotten inside your brain and really fucked you up. And you need to get well so you can see again, see that the grapes almost seem to glow, with a light dusting of some sort of powdery residue, like an incredibly light snowfall, almost as if they're covered with their own confectioners' sugar.

I wrote all this down, and then dialed the winery again. The line was still busy. Right when I hung up, a friend called and wanted to describe his latest emotional catastrophes, but I said, "No, no, talk to me about grapes." I read him what I'd written, and he said, "Yes, they really are that lovely. They do almost glow; Mother Nature wants animals to be mesmerized, hypnotized by the beauty of the fruit, so they'll eat it, shit the pits somewhere else, and make her some more." So I wrote this down on the index card, too, and I felt so happy about that card, even though I was unable to use it— until just now.

I finally got through to the winery's receptionist and told her what I needed. She said *she* always just thought of it as the wire thing, too, so she transferred me to a two-thousand-year-old monk. Or at least this is how he sounded, faint, reedy, out of breath, like Noah after a brisk walk.

And he was so glad I'd called. He actually said so, and he sounded like he was. I have secretly believed ever since that he had somehow stayed alive just long enough to be there for my phone call, and that after he answered my question, he hung up, smiled, and keeled over.

"Ah," he said, when I told him what I was after. "That would be the wire hood."

What a full day! I had a description of vineyards that could turn out to be a perfect setting for a scene somewhere down the line. I got to think about how good Mother Nature is at getting her business done, and I got to write that my character untwisted and removed the wire hood before popping the cork.

I can't tell you how many people have come up to me in the ten years since that book came out and said that they loved knowing the word for what they'd always referred to as the wire thing. Okay, the truth is I *can* tell you how many people: three. But three people who seemed genuinely pleased to have found out something they'd wondered about. Okay. Let's be honest. Two real people and my mother. Not that my mother is not a real person, but whenever I show her a copy of my latest book, she gets sort of quiet and teary, and you can tell that what she's feeling is "Oh, honey, did you make that yourself?" like it's my handprint in clay—which I suppose in many ways it is.

Writing Groups

So much of writing is about sitting down and doing it every day, and so much of it is about getting into the custom of taking in everything that comes along, seeing it all as grist for the mill. This can be a very comforting habit, like biting your nails. Instead of being scared all the time, you detach, watch what goes on, and consider it creatively. Instead of feeling panicked by those lowlifes on the subway, you notice all the details of their clothes and bearing and speech. Maybe you never quite get to the point where you think, "Ah—so that's what a gun looks like from this end." But you take in all you can, as a child would, without the atmospheric smog of most grown-up vision.

And all the while you are writing away, editing, revising, trying new leads, new endings, until finally, at some point, you want some feedback. You want other people to read it. You want to know what they think. We are social animals, and we are trying to communicate with others of our species, and up to now you have been alone in a hole getting your work done. You have no idea whether it sings to anyone but you. You wouldn't spend a month on an oil painting and then mummify it. You would hang it where people could see it. So the thought of a writing class or a writing conference may cross your mind.

Blooming writers really do not know what to expect when they sign up for a workshop or a creative-writing class. Some want to learn to write, or to write better. Others have been writing a great deal for a long time and want some feedback. These are realistic goals. A certain kind of person finds writing classes and workshops to be like camp, and just wants to hang out with all these other people, maybe with a writer he or she respects, to get and give response and encouragement, and to hear how other people tell their stories. Some people want other people with whom to share the disappointments and rejection letters and doldrums. A lot of people like to work on other people's writing because it helps them figure out what they themselves love in the written word, as well as what doesn't work for them. And others want feedback from people who aren't quite friends or editors but who will be realistic and honest and helpful.

But a lot of people come to my workshops or classes secretly hoping that I will have read their submission and absolutely flipped. I will take them aside after class and tell them that all the story needs is for them to put a little spin on the ending, maybe shorten the scene with Cammy and the ducks, and that then we'll send it off to my agent or *The New Yorker,* or maybe we'll just send it straight to Sonny Mehta. We'll *fax* it to Sonny; he would want it that way.

But I tell them that this is probably not going to happen. Every so often at a writing conference, people get taken aside by wonderful writers who love their story and who help them in some pivotal way. Every so often during one of my workshops, I'll take someone aside and say, "You're very good; work on this another six months and then give me a call, and we'll take it from there." But this is rare. Mostly what I do is listen, and encourage, and tell people what writing is like for me on a daily basis and what helps me and what doesn't. I tell people all the things I like about their piece—how wonderful the atmosphere is, for instance, and the language—and also point out where they got all tangled up in their own process. We— the other students and I—can be like a doctor to whom you take your work for a general checkup. We can give you a place to show up and a little benevolent pressure, which we hope will help you finish stories and sections. We can give you some respect, because we know what it takes.

But be warned that you may feel as though you have put your head in the lion's mouth. Creative-writing classes and ongoing workshops tend to be gentler than conferences, but in all of these situations you may find yourself sitting around a table with a number of other writers who feel morally and aesthetically compelled to rip your story to shreds. At best, they will say that the story would work better if you rewrote it in the past tense, unless it is already in the past tense, in which case they will suggest the present, or that you should try writing in the first person or, if it is in the first person, in the third. At worst, they will suggest that you have no visible talent whatsoever and should not bother writing anything ever again, even your name.

I've taught at writing conferences where students have come to me crying because the famous writer who critiqued their work that day had savaged it. I've taught at conferences where the students have been devastated by the harshness of other participants' comments, where it felt to them like the *Lord of the Flies* Writing Conference. Last summer, for instance, I was in the classroom at a huge and prestigious conference when things got completely out of hand. I sat with that day's twenty students and listened to one of them read a few pages of his work. He had not been writing for very long. It was experimental, with a lot of bad dialect, and not very good. The other students had been given his story beforehand to mark up, and when he was done, they gave him their comments. They mentioned things they liked, things they thought he had done well, moments here and there that worked. They said that the dialect had gotten in the way but that there was a great deal of heart and emotion in the story that had moved them. I thought that what they said was true, if perhaps somewhat effusive. So I said a few encouraging things, too, and pointed out a few passages that didn't ring true, recommended ways to pick up the pace, and rather gently suggested that it needed some work. The author asked a few specific questions and was given some good suggestions. Then a young woman who had been silent raised her hand.

"Am I crazy?" she implored. "Am I losing my mind? Am I the only person here who doesn't think it worked at all? Did anyone actually think there was one believable character, one meaningful image . . ." and she went on and on, while the rest of us stared at her entranced, as if frozen in cobra hypnosis. Much of what she said was true.

She looked at me when she was finished, fevered and imploring. I looked back at her. I tried to figure out what to do. There was a silence.

"Should he give up altogether?" I asked.

"I think people are patronizing him. He's not going to get better if people don't tell the truth," she wailed.

"But what you think is the truth is just your opinion."

The author of the story scanned the ceiling, as if he had heard the drone of approaching mosquitoes. The rest of the class stared at me with a sort of wired expectation. Part of me understood how the young woman felt. It had taken a lot of courage for her to speak up. And part of me wanted to tear a leg off the table and wave it at her threateningly. I knew she was a much better writer than he, because almost everyone was. I tried to breathe, and to remember what unpublished writers need and why they come to these writing conferences. They need attention. They need someone to respond to their work as honestly as possible but without being abusive or diminishing. So in my comments I focused on the fact that the author had tried something so difficult, had taken such a risk. I told him that the best possible thing was to shoot high and make mistakes, and that when he was old, or dying, he was almost certainly not going to say, "God! I'm so glad I took so few risks! I'm so glad I kept shooting so low!" I told him to plow ahead, write it one more time, and then get to work on something else.

I told the young woman, in front of the class, that it had taken guts to say what she had said. Later she sought me out and asked if I thought she was a monster. I told her I thought she'd been very honest, and that this was totally commendable, but that you don't always have to chop with the sword of truth. You can point with it, too.

Long after the conference was over, I found a poem by Bill Holm, which I wanted to send to the young man. But I no longer had his address. It is called "August in Waterton, Alberta":

> Above me, wind does its best
> to blow leaves off
> the aspen tree a month too soon.
> No use wind. All you succeed
> in doing is making music, the noise
> of failure growing beautiful.

Be aware that some conferences and writing programs can be cutthroat and competitive, and you may not need or be ready for the fiercest possible critique of your work. But if you do need feedback, encouragement, benevolent pressure, and the company of other writers, you may want to consider starting a writing group.

I've had students who met in a class of mine and who then started getting together in groups of three or four every third Thursday, or the last Sunday of the month, or whenever, and who've been doing this for years now. The fact that they're going to meet means that they have to get a certain amount of work finished. Also, an occupational hazard of writing is that you'll have bad days. You feel not only totally alone but also that everyone else is at a party. But if you talk to other people who write, you remember that this feeling is part of the process, that it's inevitable.

Writers tend to be so paranoid about talking about their work because no one, including us, really understands how it works. But it can help a great deal if you have someone you can call when you need a pep talk, someone you have learned to trust, someone who is honest and generous and who won't jinx you. When you're feeling low, you don't want anyone even to joke that you may be in some kind of astrological strike zone where you'll be for the next seven years. On a bad day you also don't need a lot of advice. You just need a little empathy and affirmation. You need to feel once again that other people have confidence in you. The members of your writing group can often offer just that.

So how do you start one? One way is to join a creative-writing class and to ask the people whose work you most love and with whom you may have some rapport if they want to begin meeting once a month, to hear and support each other's work, gossip a little, and talk about writing in general. They may say no. Then you can call Jack Kevorkian and see if he can squeeze you in. Or you can keep trying until you find two or three people who do want to see what a group would be like.

Some of my students have put ads on bulletin boards and in small newspapers, announcing the formation of a writing group for beginning writers, or for writers with novels they are trying to get published. Many, if not most, of these people have ended up with functioning groups that bring them a great deal of pleasure and support. My New Age friends claim that they've started groups by just "putting it out to the universe." Now, I *love* this sort of talk; I always picture the universe hearing the call, and flipping breathlessly through its little Rolodex, because these friends have *all* ended up in flourishing writing groups. So who's to say?

There are four people, three women and one man, who met in one of my classes and who have now been meeting as a group for four years. I see them together in bookstores or cafés, where they sit at tables with wine or coffee and go over each other's work, offer criticism and encouragement, ask questions, and figure out where to go next. They do not actually edit each other's drafts, which is something we'll talk about in the next chapter, but they listen to each other's work and help each other to keep at it.

Sometimes they'll drop in on one of my classes, like the seniors dropping by freshmen basketball practice. They end up giving the new students rousing pep talks about how great it is to be part of a writing group, how much they've come to care for one another, how it helps them get their work done. They've gone from being four tense, slightly conceited, lonely people who wanted to write to one of those weird little families we fashion out of whoever's around us. They're very tender with one another. They all look a lot less slick and cool than they did when they were in my class, because helping each other has made their hearts get bigger. A big heart is both a clunky and a delicate thing; it doesn't protect itself and it doesn't hide. It stands out, like a baby's fontanel, where you can see the soul pulse through. You can see this pulse in them now.

All four of them are excellent writers, but only one of them has been published at all, and that was just one article. But you know what? They love each other. They still look forward to their meetings after all these years. They are better writers and better people because of their work with each other. Almost always at least one of them is well and able to help, while someone else is always on the verge of giving up and dropping out of the group. But so far they have been able to talk one another into sticking it out. For instance, one of the members, the one who'd had the article published, called me last week and told me she was on the verge of giving up because she hadn't sold anything else in the months since her piece came out. She said in an Eeyore-like voice that she thought she could drink again safely now that she'd been sober for seven years, and she'd decided that I could, too, since I'd also been sober for seven years. Her plan was to come pick me and Sam up, and then we'd drive around until we found a biker bar with child care.

I made sounds of empathy and reminded her that she'd been this stuck before. Short assignments, I whispered. Shitty first drafts. She mewled. I asked if there was anyone in her writing group who might be helpful. But she said no, she couldn't call them, she knew they were all doing well, that they'd all had a great week, and that anyway they probably got together every few days without telling her and exchanged their favorite derisive stories about her and rolled their eyes.

I told her to sit down and write about how she felt, and that maybe all her loneliness and paranoia would turn out to be great material. She said she wasn't paranoid. She just worried that all her friends got together in small groups and talked meanly about her.

But right then she got a call on the other line. It turned out to be someone in her writing group who was also really depressed, and she asked me if she could call right back. Then I didn't hear from her the rest of the day. Finally I called her back, worried that she was sitting in her car in the garage with the engine running and an old Leslie Gore tape on the stereo. But it turned out that the person who'd called her was *really* on the ward, really depressed, and he is a wonderful, beautiful, funny writer who was badly abused as a child. She deeply believes in him, so she gave him a rousing pep talk, and right after hanging up, she got back to work on her book, and she had in fact been working ever since until I'd called and interrupted her.

Someone to Read Your Drafts

There's an old *New Yorker* cartoon of two men sitting on a couch at a busy cocktail party, having a quiet talk. One man has a beard and looks like a writer. The other seems like a normal person. The writer type is saying to the other, "We're still pretty far apart. I'm looking for a six-figure advance, and they're refusing to read the manuscript."

Now, I've been wrong before, but I'd bet you anything that this guy never shows his work to other writers before trying to get someone to buy it. I bet he thinks he's above that.

Whenever I'm giving a lecture at a writing conference and happen to mention the benefits of finding someone to read your drafts, at least one older established writer comes up to me and says that he or she would never in a million years show his or her work to another person before it was done. It is not a good idea, and I must stop telling my students that it will help them. I just smile, geishalike, and make little fluttery

sounds of understanding. Then I go on telling people to consider finding someone who would not mind reading their drafts
and marking them up with useful suggestions. The person may
not have an answer to what is missing or annoying about the
piece, but writing is so often about making mistakes and feeling
lost. There are probably a number of ways to tell your story
right, and someone else may be able to tell you whether or
not you've found one of these ways.

I'm not suggesting that you and another writer sit in a
cubby somewhere and write together, as though you were
doing potato prints side by side at the institution, and that
then you beam at each other's work the way you gape when
your kid first writes his name. But I am suggesting that there
may be someone out there in the world—maybe a spouse,
maybe a close friend—who will read your finished drafts and
give you an honest critique, let you know what does and
doesn't work, give you some suggestions on things you might
take out or things on which you need to elaborate, ways in
which to make your piece stronger.

In the first story of Donald Barthelme's I ever read, twenty
years ago, he said that truth is a hard apple to catch and it is
a hard apple to throw. I know what a painful feeling it is when
you've been working on something forever, and it feels done,
and you give your story to someone you hope will validate
this and that person tells you it still needs more work. You
have to, at this point, question your assessment of this person's
character and, if he or she is not a spouse or a lifelong friend,
decide whether or not you want them in your life at all. Mostly

I think an appropriate first reaction is to think that you don't. But in a little while it may strike you as a small miracle that you have someone in your life, whose taste you admire (after all, this person loves you and your work), who will tell you the truth and help you stay on the straight and narrow, or find your way back to it if you are lost.

I always show my work to one of two people before sending a copy to my editor or agent. I feel more secure and connected this way, and these two people get a lot of good work out of me. They are like midwives; there are these stories and ideas and visions and memories and plots inside me, and only I can give birth to them. Theoretically I could do it alone, but it sure makes it easier to have people helping. I have girlfriends who had their babies through natural childbirth—no drugs, no spinal, no nothing—and they secretly think they had a more honest birth experience, but I think the epidural is right up there with the most important breakthroughs in the West, like the Salk polio vaccine and salad bars in supermarkets. It's an individual thing. What works for me may not work for you. But feedback from someone I'm close to gives me confidence, or at least it gives me time to improve. Imagine that you are getting ready for a party and there is a person at your house who can check you out and assure you that you look wonderful or, conversely, that you actually do look a little tiny tiny tiny bit heavier than usual in this one particular dress or suit or that red makes you look just a bit like you have sarcoptic mange. Of course you are disappointed for a moment, but then you are grateful that you are still in the privacy of your own home and there is time to change.

One of the best writers I know has a wife who reads everything he writes and tells him when she loves it and when she doesn't, why it does or doesn't work for her. She is almost like an equal partner in the process. Two other writers I know use each other. As I said, I have two people who read my stuff. One is another writer, who is one of my best friends and probably the most neurotic, mentally ill person in my galaxy. Another is a librarian who reads two or three books a week but has never written a word. What I do is to work over a piece until it feels just about right, and then I send it to one of these two friends, who have agreed in advance to read it.

I always send my work Federal Express, because I am too impatient to wait for the mail to deliver it. I spend the entire next day waiting to hear, pacing, overeating, feeling paranoid and badly treated if I haven't heard from my friends by noon. Naturally I assume that they think it is tripe but that they don't have the courage to tell me. Then I'll think about all the things I don't like about either of them, how much in fact I hate them both, how it is no wonder that neither of them has many friends. And then the phone will ring and they usually say something along the lines of "I think it's going to be great, I think it's really good work. But I also think there are a few problems."

At this point, I am usually open to suggestion, because I'm

so relieved that they think it's going to be great. And I ask gaily where they think there's room for improvement. This is where things can get ever so slightly dicey. They might say that the whole first half is slow, and they couldn't get into it, but that on page six or thirty-eight or whatever, things finally got going, and then they couldn't put it down. They absolutely raced through the rest of it—except that maybe they had a bit of trouble with the ending, and they wonder if I really understand one character's motivation and whether I might just want to spend—oh—five minutes, no more, rethinking this person.

My first response if they have a lot of suggestions is never profound relief that I have someone in my life who will be honest with me and help me do the very best work of which I am capable. No, my first thought is, "Well. I'm sorry, but I can't be friends with you anymore, because you have too many problems. And you have a bad personality. And a bad character."

Sometimes I can't get words to come out of my mouth because I am so disappointed, as if they had said that Sam is ugly and boring and spoiled and I should let him go. Criticism is very hard to take. But then whichever friend is savaging my work will suggest that we go through it together page by page, line by line, and in a clipped, high-pitched voice I'll often suggest that this won't be necessary, that everything's just fine. But these friends usually talk me into going through the manuscript with them over the phone, and if I'll hang in there, they'll have found a number of places where things could be so much stronger, or funnier, or more real, or more interesting, or less tedious. They may even have ideas on how to fix those places, and so, by the end, I am breathing a great sigh of relief and even gratitude.

When someone reliable gives you this kind of feedback, you now have some true sense of your work's effect on people, and you may now know how to approach your final draft. If you are getting ready to send your work to a potential agent for the first time, you don't want to risk burning that bridge by sending something that's just not ready.

You really must get your piece or book just right, as right as you can. Sometimes it is just a matter of fine-tuning, or maybe one whole character needs to be rethought. Sometimes the friend will love the feel of the writing, the raw material, and yet feel that it is a million miles from being done. This can be deeply disappointing, but again, better that your spouse or friend tell you this than an agent or an editor.

I heard Marianne Williamson say once that when you ask God into your life, you think he or she is going to come into your psychic house, look around, and see that you just need a new floor or better furniture and that everything needs just a little cleaning—and so you go along for the first six months thinking how nice life is now that God is there. Then you look out the window one day and see that there's a wrecking ball outside. It turns out that God actually thinks your whole foundation is shot and you're going to have to start over from scratch. This is exactly what it can be like to give, say, a novel to someone else to read. This person can love it and still find it a total mess, in need of a great deal of work, of even a new foundation.

So how do I find one of these partners? my students ask. The same way you find a number of people for a writing group. The only difference is that in this case, you're looking for one partner instead of several. So if you are in a class, look around, see if there's someone whose work you've admired, who seems to be at about the same level as you. Then you can ask him or her if he or she wants to meet for a cup of coffee and see if you can work with each other. It's like asking for a date, so while you are doing this, you will probably be rolfed by all your most heinous memories of seventh and eighth grade. If the person says no, it's good to wait until you get inside your car before you fall apart completely. Then you can rend your clothes and keen and do a primal scream. Of course, you probably want to be sure that the person hasn't followed you out to your car. But it actually doesn't matter if he or she sees you break down, because you don't have to be friendly with that person anymore. That person is a jerk. You double up therapy sessions for a few weeks until you're back in the saddle, and then you ask someone else; someone you like much better.

If you know for sure that some smart and civilized person loves your work, you can ask that person if she would be willing to look at a part of your novel or your latest short story. If this person writes, too, ask if she would like you to take a look at her draft. If she says no to both offers, pretend to be friendly, so she won't think less of you than she already does. Then you can move into a trailer park near your therapist's house until you're well enough again to ask someone else.

The second question my students ask about a writing partner is this: what if someone agrees to read and work on your stuff for you, and you have agreed to do the same for him, say, and it turns out that he says things about your work, even in the nicest possible tone of voice, that are totally negative and destructive? You find yourself devastated, betrayed. Here you've done this incredibly gutsy thing, shown someone your very heart and soul, and he doesn't think it's any good. He says how sorry he is that this is how he feels. Well, let me tell you this—I don't think he is. I think destroying your work gave him real pleasure, pleasure he would never cop to, pleasure that is almost sexual in nature. I think you should get rid of this person immediately, even if you are married to him. No one should talk to you like this. If you write a long piece, and it is your first, and you are wondering if it's publishable, and it isn't, even by a long shot, someone should be able to tell you this in a way that is gentle yet not patronizing, so that you are encouraged—maybe not to pursue publication, but to pursue writing. Certainly this person might suggest you get a second opinion. But if he is too strident or adamant, ditch the sucker. Would you stand for someone talking this way to your children—for instance, telling them that they are not very talented at painting and shouldn't even bother? Or that their poetry is not very interesting? Of course not. You'd

169

want to go pay this person a little visit with your flamethrower. So why, if someone says something like this to you, would you want anything further to do with him? Why waste what little time you may have left with such scum?

I worry that Jesus drinks himself to sleep when he hears me talk like this. But about a month before my friend Pammy died, she said something that may have permanently changed me.

We had gone shopping for a dress for me to wear that night to a nightclub with the man I was seeing at the time. Pammy was in a wheelchair, wearing her Queen Mum wig, the *Easy Rider* look in her eyes. I tried on a lavender minidress, which is not my usual style. I tend to wear big, baggy clothes. People used to tell me I dressed like John Goodman. Anyway, the dress fit perfectly, and I came out to model it for her. I stood there feeling very shy and self-conscious and pleased. Then I said, "Do you think it makes my hips look too big?" and she said to me slowly, "Annie? I really don't think you have that kind of time."

And I don't think you have that kind of time either. I don't think you have time to waste not writing because you are afraid you won't be good enough at it, and I don't think you have time to waste on someone who does not respond to you with kindness and respect. You don't want to spend your time around people who make you hold your breath. You can't fill up when you're holding your breath. And writing is about filling up, filling up when you are empty, letting images and ideas and smells run down like water—just as writing is also

170

about dealing with the emptiness. The emptiness destroys enough writers without the help of some friend or spouse.

There are always a couple of rank beginners in my classes, and they need people to read their drafts who will rise to the occasion with respect and encouragement. Beginners always try to fit their whole lives into ten pages, and they always write blatantly about themselves, even if they make the heroine of their piece a championship racehorse with an alcoholic mother who cries a lot. But beginners are learning to play, and they need encouragement to keep their hands moving across the page.

If you look around, I think you will find the person you need. Almost every writer I've ever known has been able to find someone who could be both a friend and a critic. You'll know when the person is right for you and when you are right for that person. It's not unlike finding a mate, where little by little you begin to feel that you've stepped into a shape that was waiting there all along.

Letters

When you don't know what else to do, when you're really stuck and filled with despair and self-loathing and boredom, but you can't just leave your work alone for a while and wait, you might try telling part of your history—part of a character's history—in the form of a letter. The letter's informality just might free you from the tyranny of perfectionism.

You might address the letter to your children, if you have a few lying around, or to a niece or nephew, or to a friend. Write that person's name at the top of the page, and then in your first line, explain that you are going to tell them part of your story, entrust it to them, because this part of your life meant so much to you.

Some of the best pieces to come out of my classes have been written by people who wanted to tell their children about their own childhoods, or about their children's childhoods, what the years were like just before these children were born and then after, in that first house the family lived in, down the hill from the little white church, or about those years in the Peace Corps, in that tiny wild brilliant African village, or what it was like to work on a whaling ship in the forties. A man in one of my classes, who was raised in a family of foot-washing Baptists, wrote a two-hundred-page letter to his children about his childhood in the South, how he escaped, and his years on an Alaskan whaler, where he found God and later, in port, their mother. A woman in a class many years ago wrote a novella-length letter to her daughter about life as a Chinese American nurse living in São Paulo; it included everything she could remember having seen and felt and thought. She read part of it to our class. It was just beautiful, intimate, funny in places, and sad. People cried. Then she used it as a plot treatment for a novel.

A magazine editor recently asked me to write an essay about being a lifelong Giants fan, which I have been, but the anxiety about publication made my mind go suddenly blank. All I could remember at first was coming into the kitchen of the little coffee-colored house where I grew up to find my mother and older brother hunched over the radio listening to a Giants game with such concentration that it might have been the first news reports from Pearl Harbor. I started wanting to be able to tell Sam my stories about being a fan, because I didn't want that aspect of my life to be lost, but when I began, that one image was really all I could remember. So I started to talk to other fans about what they remembered, and it all started coming back: the whole huge bright-green overlit space that is Candlestick Park, how going there was like stepping into Oz. It was like discovering Greenland! I remembered worrying that it would surely take twenty players to cover all that land, and yet there were only three.

"Dear Sam," I wrote at the top of the page, "I want to tell you about how I loved the San Francisco Giants when I was a little kid." Instead of imagining the editor peering skeptically over my shoulder as I wrote, I pictured Sam sitting down to read this one day, how glad he might be that I had gotten it down. I started telling him my memories of the strangely reddish dirt of the base paths, the gunfire of batting practice, the feel of being part of a healthy mob, part of a pulse, part of a collective heartbeat. I called friends and compared notes about what it felt like to be a part of a huge struggle, where people were winning and losing and triumphing and being humiliated, and for once it wasn't you. Then I told Sam about this, on paper. I talked to people who remembered what it felt like to watch Juan Marichal's impossibly high kick, and Willie McCovey, the best hitter a lot of us ever saw, and Gaylord Perry with his sneaky little spitballs, so mean and snarly and sweaty that he looked like he came right out of the red-dirt country of Georgia. And then I remembered the very first time I saw Willie Mays in center field, how it was like seeing Jesus out there. I was five years old. Someone in one of my phone calls mentioned Tito Fuentes, and it all came back, how much I loved him and felt that one day we might marry, and how I loved to cry out his name along with everyone else, "Teeee-to, Teeee-to," and how it made me feel like someone from *West Side Story.*

Little by little, in telling Sam all these details, I got to see the bigger point of baseball, that it can give us back ourselves. We're a crowd animal, a highly gregarious, communicative species, but the culture and the age and all the fear that fills our days have put almost everyone into little boxes, each of us all alone. But baseball, if we love it, gives us back our place in the crowd. It restores us.

So I wrote all this down in my letter to Sam, and little by little memory and detail and fact and feeling wove themselves together. Like a Polaroid, the letter emerged, and from it the essay, clear and bright, full of smells and sounds, and full of hope, because baseball, like life, throbs with hope, or it wouldn't exist—and full of me, for Sam and his children to read one day.

Writer's Block

There are few experiences as depressing as that anxious barren state known as writer's block, where you sit staring at your blank page like a cadaver, feeling your mind congeal, feeling your talent run down your leg and into your sock. Or you look at the notes you've scribbled recently on yellow legal pads or index cards, and they look like something Richard Speck jotted down the other night. And at the same time, as it turns out, you happen to know that your closest writing friend is on a roll, has been turning out stories and screenplays and children's books and even most of a novel like he or she is some crazy pot-holder factory, pot holders pouring out the windows because there is simply not enough room inside for such glorious productivity.

Writer's block is going to happen to you. You will read what little you've written lately and see with absolute clarity that it is total dog shit. A blissfully productive manic stage may come to a screeching halt, and all of a sudden you realize you're Wile E. Coyote and you've run off the cliff and are a second away from having to look down. Or else you haven't been able to write anything at all for a while. The fear that you'll never write again is going to hit you when you feel not only lost and unable to find a few little bread crumbs that would identify the path you were on but also when you're at your lowest ebb of energy and faith. You may feel a little as if writing a novel is like trying to level Mount McKinley with a dentist's drill. Things feel hopeless, or at least bleak, and you are not imaginative or organized enough to bash your way through to a better view, let alone some interesting conclusion. You know where every idea, quote, and image came from; none of them is fresh. You're so familiar with what you're saying that your words all sound utterly commonplace. Writers are like vacuum cleaners, sucking up all that we can see and hear and read and think and feel and articulate, and everything that everyone else within earshot can hear and see and think and feel. We're mimics, we're parrots—we're writers. But knowing the source of all our stuff deprives it of its magic, because then the material feels mundane, clichéd; you didn't have to discover it because it was already there for all to see. You may start to feel that you are trying to pass off a TV dinner as home cooking.

We have all been there, and it feels like the end of the world. It's like a little chickadee being hit by an H-bomb. Here's the thing, though. I no longer think of it as block. I think that is looking at the problem from the wrong angle. If your wife locks you out of the house, you don't have a problem with your door.

The word *block* suggests that you are constipated or stuck, when the truth is that you're empty. As I said in the last chapter, this emptiness can destroy some writers, as do the shame and frustration that go with it. You feel that the writing gods gave you just so many good days, maybe even enough of them to write one good book and then part of another. But now you are having some days or weeks of emptiness, as if suddenly the writing gods are saying, "Enough! Don't bother me! I have given to you until it hurts! Please. I've got problems of my own."

The problem is acceptance, which is something we're taught not to do. We're taught to improve uncomfortable situations, to change things, alleviate unpleasant feelings. But if you accept the reality that you have been given—that you are not in a productive creative period—you free yourself to begin filling up again. I encourage my students at times like these to get one page of anything written, three hundred words of memories or dreams or stream of consciousness on how much they hate writing—just for the hell of it, just to keep their fingers from becoming too arthritic, just because they have made a commitment to try to write three hundred words every day. Then, on bad days and weeks, let things go at that.

◆ ◆ ◆

I remind myself nearly every day of something that a doctor told me six months before my friend Pammy died. This was a doctor who always gave me straight answers. When I called on this one particular night, I was hoping she could put a positive slant on some distressing developments. She couldn't, but she said something that changed my life. "Watch her carefully right now," she said, "because she's teaching you how to live."

I remind myself of this when I cannot get any work done: to live as if I am dying, because the truth is we are all terminal on this bus. To live as if we are dying gives us a chance to experience some real presence. Time is so full for people who are dying in a conscious way, full in the way that life is for children. They spend big round hours. So instead of staring miserably at the computer screen trying to will my way into having a breakthrough, I say to myself, "Okay, hmmm, let's see. Dying tomorrow. What should I do today?" Then I can decide to read Wallace Stevens for the rest of the morning or go to the beach or just really participate in ordinary life. Any of these will begin the process of filling me back up with observations, flavors, ideas, visions, memories. I might want to write on my last day on earth, but I'd also be aware of other options that would feel at least as pressing. I would want to keep whatever I did simple, I think. And I would want to be present.

◆ ◆ ◆

In the beginning, when you're first starting out, there are a million reasons not to write, to give up. That is why it is of extreme importance to make a commitment to finishing sections and stories, to driving through to the finish. The discouraging voices will hound you—"This is all piffle," they will say, and they may be right. What you are doing may just be practice. But this is how you are going to get better, and there is no point in practicing if you don't finish.

I went through a real crisis of faith about two-thirds of the way through my last novel. The thing is that I had gotten twenty-seven bad reviews in a row on my previous novel, and I was feeling just the merest bit unsure about my skills and the joys of publication. But during that crisis of faith, I made a commitment to the characters in the new novel, instead of to the book itself. So I spent a little time at my desk every day, just writing down memories of my family, my youth. I went for walks and to lots of matinees, and I read. I spent as much time as I could outdoors while I waited for my unconscious to open a door and beckon.

It finally did. I did not have some beautiful Hallmark moment when I threw back my shoulders with a big smile, dusted off my old hands, and got back to work. Rather, it was like catching amoebic dysentery. I was just sitting there minding my business, and then the next minute I rushed to my desk with an urgency I had not believed possible.

It helps to resign as the controller of your fate. All that energy we expend to keep things running right is not what's keeping things running right. We're bugs struggling in the river, brightly visible to the trout below. With that fact in mind, people like me make up all these rules to give us the illusion that we are in charge. I need to say to myself, they're not needed, hon. Just take in the buggy pleasures. Be kind to the others, grab the fleck of riverweed, notice how beautifully your bug legs scull.

All the good stories are out there waiting to be told in a fresh, wild way. Mark Twain said that Adam was the only man who, when he said a good thing, knew that nobody had said it before. Life is like a recycling center, where all the concerns and dramas of humankind get recycled back and forth across the universe. But what you have to offer is your own sensibility, maybe your own sense of humor or insider pathos or meaning. All of us can sing the same song, and there will still be four billion different renditions. Some people will sing it spontaneously, with a lot of soulful riffs, while others are going to practice until they could sing it at the Met. Either way, everything we need in order to tell our stories in a reasonable and exciting way already exists in each of us. Everything you need is in your head and memories, in all that your senses provide, in all that you've seen and thought and absorbed. There in your unconscious, where the real creation goes on, is the little kid or the Dr. Seuss creature in the cellar, arranging and stitching things together. When this being is ready to hand things up to you, to give you a paragraph or a sudden move one character makes that will change the whole course of your novel, you will be entrusted with it. So, in the meantime, while the tailor is working, you might as well go get some fresh air. Do your three hundred words, and then go for a walk. Otherwise you'll want to sit there and try to contribute, and this will only get in the way. Your unconscious can't work when you are breathing down its neck. You'll sit there going, "Are you done in there yet, are you done in there yet?" But it is trying to tell you nicely, "Shut up and go away."

Part Four

Publication— and Other Reasons to Write

Writing a Present

Publication is not going to change your life or solve your problems. Publication will not make you more confident or more beautiful, and it will probably not make you any richer. There will be a very long buildup to publication day, and then the festivities will usually be over rather quickly. We will talk about all of this at great length shortly. In the meantime, let's discuss some of the other reasons to write that may surprise a writer, even a writer who hasn't given up on getting published. There are arenas full of potential for rich reward, where your life and your sense of self and of abundance really can be changed. (All of a sudden I cannot remember if we are allowed to use the word *abundance* in California anymore. I will have to get back to you on this.)

Twice now I have written books that began as presents to people I loved who were going to die. I've told you a little about my father's diagnosis of brain cancer, how all of a sudden

I had a sad story to tell. It was a story rich with drama and humor, about a father and his three semigrown children living in a tiny town filled with aging hippies, trust-fund radicals, artists, New Agers, and ordinary people, whatever that means. Out of nowhere, the rug was suddenly pulled out from under the family, when it looked as if the father had a terminal illness and was actually going to go ahead and die.

So I started writing about our new life. I recorded moments of my brothers trying to help our father, trying to help one another, all of us trying to keep our senses of humor, trying to find meaning in it all, and saying what was really on our minds. There were lots of descriptions of the townspeople and the landscape that I'd already written that I still liked and could use. But the best stuff was what my father and brothers were going through right then, right at that moment. I scribbled down the funny things they said, the tender moments, the black humor, the weirdness of it all. Then I started shaping that material into self-contained stories. I showed them to my father, who thought it was great that all this pain and fear and loss were being transformed into a story of love and survival. He would hand me back my pages, raise his fist in the black-power salute, and smile. This was enough to keep me going. In a sense, I was giving him a love letter. He never got his version of the story written, but the miracle was that I finished mine while his brain was still working. He got to read the whole thing. He got to know that he and his story were going to exist long after he took off his dog suit and went to the great beyond.

Another propellant for this first novel of mine was that I found myself desperate for books that talked about cancer in a way that would both illuminate the experience and make me laugh. But there weren't very many. In fact, there was only one that I was aware of, Violet Weingarten's *Intimations of Mortality,* a journal of her chemotherapy, from which I got my book's epigram: "Is life too short to be taking shit, or is life too short to be minding it?" I read the book over and over, read it out loud to my brothers over the phone, then went to the library and said, "Do you have any other really funny books about cancer?" And they looked at me like, Yeah, they're right over there by the comedies about spina bifida. There didn't seem to be any. A book about our experience, showing one family's attempt to stay buoyant in the face of such a potentially flattening process, seemed like it might be a welcome present to other people with sick relatives. This is all I tried to do, to tell our family's story, because with an enormous amount of support from friends, there were laughter and joy folded into all that fear and loss. It helped my father have the best possible months before his death and the best possible death. I can actually say that it was great. Hard, and fucked six ways from Sunday, but great.

Of course, not everyone loved my book. There were some terrible reviews. My personal favorite was from a newspaper in Santa Barbara, which said that our black sense of humor made us look like a New Age Addams family. "Here's your review from Santa Barbara," my editor wrote on a note enclosed with it, "where people never die."

Fifteen years later my friend Pammy was diagnosed with breast cancer. I had been keeping a journal about my new son, whom she was helping me raise, so most of the journal entries already included her. And now all of a sudden it turned out that she was not going to be around for much longer. So I started typing up the journal entries and sending them off to my agent. Sam was getting bigger and Pammy was getting sicker, and I was writing as fast as I could, trying to get it done in time for her to read it. And I did. I gave her a finished copy four months before she died. It was another love letter, mostly to her and Sam, and for her daughter, Rebecca. Pammy knew there was something that was going to exist on paper after she was gone, something that was going to be, in a certain way, part of her immortality.

Again, there was a part of me that believed that my journal could be a gift for others, for single mothers. I couldn't find any books about single parenting when Sam was first born that were funny and sick and therefore true. There were some great books on child rearing, but none that made me laugh, and none that went into the dark side, the *Seventh-Seal*-with-milky-bras part. They were all so nicey-nice and rational and suggested that surely if you did this or that, the colicky little darling would come around, pull himself or herself together, get a grip. And this simply wasn't true. Having a baby is like suddenly getting the world's worst roommate, like having Janis Joplin with a bad hangover and PMS come to stay with you. All the available baby books recommended things like white noise to soothe the yowling little savant. So I'd sit there by

Sam's side and play him Sierra Club tapes of rivers at night, complete with crickets and owls and frogs, and he'd look over worriedly for a moment, like "Are you out of your mind? Why don't you just play me a tape of shark fights?" And then he would *really* start to cry.

I would have felt so relieved if there had been a book written by another mother who admitted that she sometimes wanted to grab her infant by the ankles and swing him over her head like a bolo. So I went ahead and started writing one myself, as a present, as a kind of road map for other mothers.

I would have been so relieved, too, if after Pammy got sick when Sam was eight months old, there had been a book about losing your best friend that was real but also funny. So I ended up trying to write one, weaving together these two stories, of Sam and Pammy, for both of them and for anyone who might know anyone like either of them.

A couple of years later, a few months after Pammy died, two close friends of ours had a baby who was born so damaged that he died at five months old. I began to wonder if I was some sort of carrier. Sam and I spent a lot of time with the parents and their little son. They did such an amazing job and taught me so much, and their son taught me so much that I wanted other people to know about it. I wanted to write about it as a present for the parents, so that this baby would keep on living. So all those months when Brice was alive, I scribbled down notes on index cards, with no idea of whether I would ever actually write a story about him. I watched all that went

...side me: how I automatically think that closing down is safe, but that really staying open and loving is safer, because then we're connected to all that life and love. And I watched Sam watch Brice and scribbled some of this down on index cards. I felt self-conscious and vaguely ashamed that so much of what I'd written lately concerned suffering and death, but I let myself take notes anyway.

Brice died that May. A month or so later I had the opportunity to write a three-minute essay for a radio show on anything I wanted, and I asked Brice's parents if it would feel like an invasion of privacy if I wrote about their son. They said no, just the opposite. So I sat down with my index cards, and I looked through the one-inch picture frame, and started writing:

Sam saw his first dead person last month. Two friends of ours had a baby who died, and we went to spend the morning with them and the body of their son. He was five months old and weighed eight pounds, down from the ten he weighed at birth. He wore a white baptismal gown, and lay in a big basket on top of his crib, covered with flower petals from the waist down, white as a rose. There were flowers and shrines everywhere, statues of the Buddha and pictures of his Holiness the Dalai Lama (because his mother is a Buddhist) and of Jesus (because his father is a Christian). Brice looked like a small, concerned angel from someplace snowy. None of us, including Sam, could take our eyes off him. He looked like God.

"You what?" my relatives asked when I mentioned this. "You

took Sam to see what?" as in, What will you take him to see next? Brain surgery? I couldn't explain why I thought it was right, except that I was taught to be terrified of sickness and death (especially early death and also, ironically, aging) and I believe this greatly compromised my life. Of course I want better for Sam.

Lots of my friends have died of cancer and AIDS. But Brice was the first dead person Sam ever saw. Sam didn't seem scared. Maybe it was because Brice looked so beautiful in death. He was an old pro at it: he had died during delivery and was resuscitated seven minutes later, and so was born a second time, but it turned out that he had been gone too long. His eyes were deep gray, and always open, and he never cried or, for that matter, smiled, or even blinked.

Brice's mother's Buddhist friends called him Cloud Boy because he was suspended between heaven and earth, not quite here, not quite there. His father's Christian friends did much of the cooking. Everyone held him and rocked him. Sam and I spent a lot of time reading to him, mostly Dr. Seuss.

"He's a good baby," Sam assured Brice's parents one day. Not knowing how on earth they would take care of him, they had brought Brice home when he was three weeks old, because they didn't want him to die at the hospital. They just wanted him to be home with them and their friends. It was an amazing thing to be a part of. Some people saw Brice as a tragedy, thought his parents were crazy for not leaving him at the hospital. The rest of us felt incredibly sad but also that maybe we were in the presence of something holy, something that didn't have to do with personality or character or age.

"He's a good *baby*," Sam told me one day in the car, after we'd been reading to Brice for a while. "But he's a little funky."

When Brice died, his parents called us and asked if Sam and I would come over. They were sad but Okay. Sam brought the baby two presents that morning, which he laid in the basket. One was a ball, in case you get to play catch on the other side. The other was a small time-travel car, from Back to the Future. Brice's parents and I are still scratching our heads over that one.

After we left that morning, I took Sam to the local bowling lanes. It was another big first for him. It was all so ridiculous and real that it felt sort of sacred. We bowled in the kids' lane for an hour. "You took him *where?*" asked my relatives. And I couldn't really explain why. It had something to do with wanting to shake off the solemnity, with wanting to complete the cycle of life and death. Bowling is life at its most immediate—you fling a ball and the pins fall down, sometimes. And I also wanted to show Sam that the holy goes on, no matter how many balls you fling at it.

I read this to Brice's parents before I read it on the radio, and then they called everyone they knew and told them when it would be on, and they recorded it. And even though their son will always be alive in their hearts, like Pammy and my dad will be alive in mine—and maybe this is the only way we ever really have anyone—there is still something to be said for painting portraits of the people we have loved, for trying to express those moments that seem so inexpressibly beautiful, the ones that change us and deepen us.

◆ ◆ ◆

Toni Morrison said, "The function of freedom is to free someone else," and if you are no longer wracked or in bondage to a person or a way of life, tell your story. Risk freeing someone else. Not everyone will be glad that you did. Members of your family and other critics may wish you had kept your secrets. Oh, well, what are you going to do? Get it all down. Let it pour out of you onto the page. Write an incredibly shitty, self-indulgent, whiny, mewling first draft. Then take out as many of the excesses as you can.

One thing I haven't told you about my famous short story "Arnold" is that besides sending it off every few months to my father's agent, I also sent it off to an important magazine editor. He sent it back with the following note: "You have made the mistake of thinking that everything that has happened to you is interesting." Now, needless to say, I was mortified. But the note ended up only helping me because it didn't stop me. Still, I sat down with great trepidation when I began to write the story of my father's illness, because of the mistake this editor said I had made, which I *had* made. And I tried very hard not to make it again. So first I wrote down everything that happened to us, and then I took out the parts that felt self-indulgent. I wasn't writing the book with my thumb stuck out, trying to hitchhike into history: I just wanted to write a book for my father that might also help someone going through a similar situation. Some people may have thought that this book was too personal, too confessional. But what these people think about me is none of my business. I got to write books about my father and my best friend, and they got to read them before they died. Can you imagine? I wrote for an audience of two whom I loved and respected, who loved and respected me. So I wrote for them as carefully and soulfully as I could—which is, needless to say, how I wish I could write all the time.

Finding Your Voice

I heard a tape once in which an actor talked about trying to find God in the modern world and how, left to our own devices, we seek instead all the worldly things—possessions, money, looks, and power—because we think they will bring us fulfillment. But this turns out to be a joke, because they are just props, and when we check out of this life, we have to give them all back to the great propmaster in the sky. "They're just on loan," he said. "They're not ours." This tape changed how I felt about my students emulating their favorite writers. It helped me see that it is natural to take on someone else's style, that it's a prop that you use for a while until you have to give it back. And it just might take you to the thing that is not on loan, the thing that is real and true: your own voice.

I often ask my students to scribble down in class the reason they want to write, why they are in my class, what is propelling them to do this sometimes-excruciating, sometimes-boring work. And over and over, they say in effect, "I will not be silenced again." They were good children, who often felt invisible and who saw some awful stuff. But at some point they stopped telling what they saw because when they did, they were punished. Now they want to look at their lives—at life— and they don't want to be sent to their rooms for doing so. But it is very hard to find their own voice and it is tempting to assume someone else's.

Every time Isabel Allende has a new book out, I'm happy because I will get to read it, and I'm unhappy because half of my students are going to start writing like her. Now, I love Ms. Allende's work, as I love a number of South and Central American writers. When I read their books, I feel like I'm sitting around a campfire at night where they are spinning their wild stories—these crazy Rube Goldberg clocks, with lots of birds and maidens and gongs and bells and whistles. I understand why this style is so attractive to my students: it's like primitive art. It's simple and decorative, with rich colors, satisfying old forms, and a lot of sophistication underneath that you feel but don't really see. I always feel like I'm watching a wild theater piece with lots of special effects—so many lives falling apart! But, more important, this style offers the nourishment of imagination and wonder. I love to enter into these fantastical worlds where we feel like we're looking through the wrong end of the binoculars, where everything is tiny and pretty and rich, because real life is so often big and messy and hurtful and drab. But when someone like Allende polishes and turns and twists her people and their lives and their families and their ghosts into universal curves and shapes, then the writing resonates in such a way that you think, Yes, yes, that's exactly what life is like.

I love for my students to want to have this effect. But their renditions never ring true, any more than they ring true a few months later when Ann Beattie's latest book arrives and my students start submitting stories about shiny bowls and windowpanes. We do live our lives on surfaces, and Beattie does surfaces beautifully, burnishing them, bringing out the details. But when my students do Beattie, their stories tend to be lukewarm, and I say to them, Life is lukewarm enough! Give us a little heat! If I'm going to read about a bunch of people who drive Volkswagens and seem to have mostly Volkswagen-sized problems, and the writer shows them driving around on top of the ice, I want a sense that there's a lot of very, very cold water down below. I eventually want for someone to crash through. I want people who write to crash or dive below the surface, where life is so cold and confusing and hard to see. I want writers to plunge through the holes—the holes we try to fill up with all the props. In those holes and in the spaces around them exist all sorts of possibility, including the chance to see who we are and to glimpse the mystery.

The great writers keep writing about the cold dark place within, the water under a frozen lake or the secluded, camouflaged hole. The light they shine on this hole, this pit, helps us cut away or step around the brush and brambles; then we can dance around the rim of the abyss, holler into it, measure it, throw rocks in it, and still not fall in. It can no longer swallow us up. And we can get on with things.

A sober friend once said to me, "When I was still drinking, I was a sedated monster. After I got sober, I was just a monster." He told me about his monster. His sounded just like mine without quite so much mascara. When people shine a little light on their monster, we find out how similar most of our monsters are. The secrecy, the obfuscation, the fact that these monsters can only be hinted at, gives us the sense that they must be very bad indeed. But when people let their monsters out for a little onstage interview, it turns out that we've all done or thought the same things, that this is our lot, our condition. We don't end up with a brand on our forehead. Instead, we compare notes.

We write to expose the unexposed. If there is one door in the castle you have been told not to go through, you must. Otherwise, you'll just be rearranging furniture in rooms you've already been in. Most human beings are dedicated to keeping that one door shut. But the writer's job is to see what's behind it, to see the bleak unspeakable stuff, and to turn the un-speakable into words—not just into any words but if we can, into rhythm and blues.

You can't do this without discovering your own true voice, and you can't find your true voice and peer behind the door and report honestly and clearly to us if your parents are reading over your shoulder. They are probably the ones who told you not to open that door in the first place. You can tell if they're there because a small voice will say, "Oh, whoops, don't say that, that's a secret," or "That's a bad word," or "Don't tell anyone you jack off. They'll all start doing it." So you have to breathe or pray or do therapy to send them away. Write as if your parents are dead. As I've said, we will discuss libel later in this book.

"Why, though?" my students ask, staring at me intently. "Why are we supposed to open all these doors? Why are we supposed to tell the truth in our own voice?" And I stare back at them for a moment. I guess because it's our nature, I say. Also, I think that most of your characters believe, as children believe, that if the truth were known, they would be seen as good people. Truth seems to want expression. Unacknowledged truth saps your energy and keeps you and your characters wired and delusional. But when you open the closet door and let what was inside out, you can get a rush of liberation and even joy. If we can believe in the Gnostic gospel of Thomas, old Uncle Jesus said, "If you bring forth what is inside you, what you bring forth will save you. If you don't bring forth what is inside you, what you bring forth can destroy you."

And the truth of your experience can *only* come through in your own voice. If it is wrapped in someone else's voice, we readers will feel suspicious, as if you are dressed up in someone else's clothes. You cannot write out of someone else's big dark place; you can only write out of your own. Sometimes wearing someone else's style is very comforting, warm and pretty and bright, and it can loosen you up, tune you into the joys of language and rhythm and concern. But what you say will be an abstraction because it will not have sprung from direct experience: when you try to capture the truth of your experience in some other person's voice or on that person's terms, you are removing yourself one step further from what you have seen and what you know.

Truth, or reality, or whatever you want to call it is the bedrock of life. A black man at my church who is nearing one hundred thundered last Sunday, "*God* is your home," and I pass this on mostly because all of the interesting characters I've ever worked with—including myself—have had at their center a feeling of otherness, of homesickness. And it's wonderful to watch someone finally open that forbidden door that has kept him or her away. What gets exposed is not people's baseness but their humanity. It turns out that the truth, or reality, is our home.

Look at the two extremes. Maybe you find truth in Samuel Beckett—that we're very much alone and it's all scary and annoying and it smells like dirty feet and the most you can hope for is that periodically someone will offer a hand or a rag or a tiny word of encouragement just when you're going under. The redemption in Beckett is so small: in the second act of *Waiting for Godot,* the barren dying twig of a tree has put out a leaf. Just one leaf. It's not much; still Beckett didn't commit suicide. He wrote.

Or maybe truth as you understand it is 180 degrees away— that God is everywhere and we are all where we're supposed to be and more will be revealed one day. Maybe you feel that

Wordsworth was right, maybe Rumi, maybe Stephen Mitchell writing on Job: "The physical body is acknowledged as dust, the personal drama as delusion. It is as if the world we perceive through our senses, that whole gorgeous and terrible pageant, were the breath-thin surface of a bubble, and everything else, inside and outside, is pure radiance. Both suffering and joy come then like a brief reflection, and death like a pin."

But you can't get to any of these truths by sitting in a field smiling beatifically, avoiding your anger and damage and grief. Your anger and damage and grief are the way to the truth. We don't have much truth to express unless we have gone into those rooms and closets and woods and abysses that we were told not to go in to. When we have gone in and looked around for a long while, just breathing and finally taking it in—then we will be able to speak in our own voice and to stay in the present moment. And that moment is home.

G i v i n g

Annie Dillard has said that day by day you have to give the
work before you all the best stuff you have, not saving up for
later projects. If you give freely, there will always be more.
This is a radical proposition that runs so contrary to human
nature, or at least to my nature, that I personally keep trying
to find loopholes in it. But it is only when I go ahead and
decide to shoot my literary, creative wad on a daily basis that
I get any sense of full presence, of being Zorba the Greek at
the keyboard. Otherwise I am a wired little rodent squirreling
things away, hoarding and worrying about supply. Arthritis
forms in my hands and in the hands my mind is using to shape
things, in the hands of that creature in the cellar who wants
and needs to use all of his favorite rags in the ragbag he works
from.

You are going to have to give and give and give, or there's

no reason for you to be writing. You have to give from the deepest part of yourself, and you are going to have to go on giving, and the giving is going to have to be its own reward. There is no cosmic importance to your getting something published, but there is in learning to be a giver.

Your work as a writer, when you are giving everything you have to your characters and to your readers, will periodically make you feel like the single parent of a three-year-old, who is, by turns, wonderful, willful, terrible, crazed, and adoring. Toddlers can make you feel as if you have violated some archaic law in their personal Koran and you should die, infidel. Other times they'll reach out and touch you like adoring grandparents on their deathbeds, trying to memorize your face with their fingers. One night I was lying in bed with Sam when he was about three and a half, and he touched my cheeks tenderly, as if they were sunburned. "I love that little face," he said, and I felt like in a moment he might squeeze my cheeks and exclaim, "Mein shayner punim!" *My beautiful face.*

And then the next day Sam was treating me like I was the bunny at his own private Playboy Club and he had run out of drinks half an hour before.

But they are always yours, your books as well as your children. You helped bring your work into being, and every day you have to feed it, help it stay well, give it advice and love it when it ignores you.

Your three-year-old and your work in progress teach you to give. They teach you to get out of yourself and become a person for someone else. This is probably the secret to happiness. So that's one reason to write. Your child and your work hold you hostage, suck you dry, ruin your sleep, mess with your head, treat you like dirt, and then you discover they've given you that gold nugget you were looking for all along.

Two things put me in the spirit to give. One is that I have come to think of almost everyone with whom I come into contact as a patient in the emergency room. I see a lot of gaping wounds and dazed expressions. Or, as Marianne Moore put it, "The world's an orphan's home." And this feels more true than almost anything else I know. But so many of us can be soothed by writing: think of how many times you have opened a book, read *one* line, and said, "Yes!" And I want to give people that feeling, too, of connection, communion.

The other is to think of the writers who have given a book to me, and then to write a book back to them. This gift they have given us, which we pass on to those around us, was fashioned out of their lives. You wouldn't be a writer if reading hadn't enriched your soul more than other pursuits. So write a book back to V. S. Naipaul or Margaret Atwood or Wendell Berry or whoever it is who most made you want to write, whose work you most love to read. Make it as good as you can. It is one of the greatest feelings known to humans, the feeling of being the host, of hosting people, of being the person to whom they come for food and drink and company. This is what the writer has to offer.

◆ ◆ ◆

Here is the best true story on giving I know, and it was told by Jack Kornfield of the Spirit Rock Meditation Center in Woodacre. An eight-year-old boy had a younger sister who was dying of leukemia, and he was told that without a blood transfusion she would die. His parents explained to him that his blood was probably compatible with hers, and if so, he could be the blood donor. They asked him if they could test his blood. He said sure. So they did and it was a good match. Then they asked if he would give his sister a pint of blood, that it could be her only chance of living. He said he would have to think about it overnight.

The next day he went to his parents and said he was willing to donate the blood. So they took him to the hospital where he was put on a gurney beside his six-year-old sister. Both of them were hooked up to IVs. A nurse withdrew a pint of blood from the boy, which was then put in the girl's IV. The boy lay on his gurney in silence while the blood dripped into his sister, until the doctor came over to see how he was doing. Then the boy opened his eyes and asked, "How soon until I start to die?"

Sometimes you have to be that innocent to be a writer. Writing takes a combination of sophistication and innocence; it takes conscience, our belief that something is beautiful because it's right. To be great, art has to point somewhere. So if you are no longer familiar with that place of naive conscience, it's hard to see any point in your being a writer. Almost all of my close friends are walking personality disorders, but I know innocence is in them because I can see it in their faces and in their decisions. I can almost promise that this quality is still in you, that you are capable of quiet heroism.

This sophisticated innocence is a gift. It is yours to give away. We are wired as humans to be open to the world instead of enclosed in a fortified, defensive mentality. What your giving can do is to help your readers be braver, be better than they are, be open to the world again. One does not need to be optimistic in order to do this. My priest friend, Rankin, for instance, describes himself as a cheerful pessimist, and this attitude is enough to rescue him from the bleakness that would otherwise have him psychically curled up in the fetal position.

Now, come to think of it, this autism is a great position for one of your characters to end up in near the climax, because the killing of this deadness is a great theme. In real life, most people don't actually curl up in the fetal position in order to tune out their feelings. Most people get strung out on relationships with other people or on work or drugs or alcohol or food. But a similar trance is induced.

You may find that your character is not well enough for this deadness to be killed or, at least, not ready yet. Heaven knows, punishment and trance are a great deal more comfortable and familiar than aliveness. It's like that old joke about denial. A woman goes to the zoo and is completely taken by the beauty and power of the gorilla. She cannot take her eyes off him. He is sleeping against the bars of the cage, and even though a sign says not to, she reaches her hand in to stroke him. Instantly, he awakes and goes berserk, tearing the bars of the cage open to get at her, mauling her to within an inch of her life. Finally, the zoo personnel manage to hit him with the tranquilizer darts. The woman is taken to an ICU, barely alive, but slowly, slowly she pulls through. After four days she is finally allowed visitors. Her best friend arrives. The woman can barely open her eyes. "God, you look like you're in a lot of pain," the friend says, and the woman sighs. "Pain," she says. "You don't know pain. He doesn't call, he doesn't write . . ."

This is one of my favorite jokes because the character is so familiar to me. She is probably familiar to a lot of people you know. Maybe she is not ready for the deadness to be killed, or maybe, against all odds, she is. Maybe you can give her something from deep within to find or do or fight for that will break the trance for her. You'll have to find this first within you, though. And then you'll have it to give away. This woman may get to wake up. And then she will have something to give, a song to sing. Maybe it won't be a song exactly, but maybe just a little tune, a calliope tune, the tune of survival.

Publication

All right, let's talk about publication. Let's talk about the myth of publication.

Say you've finished your book, or a draft of the book, or a whole lot of stories, and you send them off to your agent, if you have one, or to a friend's agent, or to an agent you've found listed in the Yellow Pages or in the *Literary Market Place*. Say you actually already *have* an editor somewhere, or an editor who once wrote you an admiring rejection letter, so you send your book or stories to him or her and to a couple of friends. As I've mentioned, I'm one of those people who feels beside herself the day after I've stuck the manuscript in the mail. It can't have even arrived and already I'm feeling bitter and resentful about what cold, lazy, sadistic slime I'm surrounded by. There are other writers, and you may be one of them, who just push back their sleeves and get to work on the next piece. I could never be close to a person like this, but I know they exist. Anyway, if you are like me, you wait and wait and check your mail ten times each day, and feel devastated and rejected every hour that there is no response. Finally, if you are lucky, a week later you get a note from your agent's assistant that the manuscript has in fact arrived, and maybe one of the friends has called to say that he or she has read part of it and that it is just terrific and not to worry, but you go ahead and have a small breakdown anyhow, waiting for your agent and editor to call and tell you that it's brilliant. Every time the phone rings, you sing, "Let it please be him, oh, dear God, it *must* be him." But it's not him, and then you die and go on a massive eating binge and think about what phonies most of your friends are. And then you calm down. You go for a walk. You're a little better. Then you try to read something, but you end up reading your own manuscript and reeling with shame at how bad it is. But just when you start to go into actual spasm, your friend calls back and says he's just read another chapter and really, on the souls of his grandchildren, he swears it's the best thing you've ever written; he loves it and he loves you.

So you are Okay again, for a good ten minutes or so.

After another week, you call your agent because you can't stand pretending to be cool anymore, but your agent hasn't read your manuscript yet because he is swamped with infinitely more important matters. He tells you with the faintest hint of irritation that the very second he finishes it or hears from your editor, you will be called. And that everything is probably just fine. Okay? the agent asks. All better? You want to go rip his face off. Instead, you pray.

And then you see in a flash of blinding insight that your agent and editor are in cahoots, and what you heard as irritation was really just the strain of withholding hysterics. After being on the phone all morning reading each other passages from your book, they agree that it is the most embarrassingly bad book ever written, and they are honking and screaming with laughter. At one point your editor is laughing so hard that she has to take some digitalis, and your agent ruptures a blood vessel in his throat. They are reading the scene to each other where your hero's father dies.

(And if you actually have a contract with these people, you assume that your editor has to get off the phone at this point so that he can go talk to the legal department to see if they have to pay you the last part of the advance they owe you, or if maybe they can even sue you to collect the money they have already paid you.)

But all you can do is wait and wait and wait, until finally your agent or editor calls and says the book is terrific and it will be published in the spring or the fall or whenever. It will be published. And then there are some happy months, re-writing, editing, working with the copy editor, loved and reassured every step of the way, and then there is the utter miracle of galleys, where your book comes to you set in type and it looks like a real person was involved in writing it.

Many nonwriters assume that publication is a thunderously

joyous event in the writer's life, and it is certainly the biggest and brightest carrot dangling before the eyes of my students. They believe that if they themselves were to get something published, their lives would change instantly, dramatically, and for the better. Their self-esteem would flourish; all self-doubt would be erased like a typo. Entire paragraphs and manuscripts of disappointment and rejection and lack of faith would be wiped out by one push of a psychic delete button and replaced by a quiet, tender sense of worth and belonging. Then they could wrap the world in flame.

But this is not exactly what happens. Or at any rate, this is not what it has been like for me.

For me, it has been more like a cross between the last few weeks of pregnancy, when you look and feel like Orson Welles and you are hormonally challenged up the yang, your ankles are swollen and you feel revulsion at the smell of vegetables cooking; and the first day of seventh-grade PE class, when they make you line up by size before they hand out your gym uniform. And you're either four feet tall, like E.T., or made to feel like Diane Arbus's Jewish giant.

Oh, the process starts off well enough. One day several months before your pub date, you get a set of bound galleys, which is to say, a paperbound book with your manuscript set in type. I always feel a desperate sense of relief at this point, because it seems like the publisher is too far in now to cancel publication. These bound galleys have also gone out to hundreds of papers and reviewers, and this makes you believe that the publisher has already shelled out so much money in production and postage costs that they will have to go ahead and actually publish the damn thing.

The first time you read through your galleys is heaven. The second time through, all you see are the typos no one caught. It looks like the typesetter typed it with frostbitten feet, drunk. And the typos are important ones. They make you look ignorant; they make you look like an ignorant racist. By the third or fourth time through, you can see that there is not one fresh or insightful or even salvageable line in the whole thing. By the fifth reading, you are no longer sure that publishing this would be in your best interests.

Not long after, you get your early reviews, in *Publishers Weekly* and *Kirkus Reviews,* and sometimes they sound like your mother wrote them. Other times they suggest that you are a show-offy vacuous loser, and they hope you die so that they won't have to read your work anymore. I have gotten prepub reviews that said I was a treadmark on the underpants of life. Perhaps this is not exactly what they said, but by reading between the lines, I could see that this is what they were implying. You survive that. Possibly you're still drinking, so you have a pitcher of martinis just to take the edge off, or you've quit drinking, so you eat your body weight in pastries and Mexican food. Somehow you get the time to pass, and then your pub date arrives.

There is something mythic about the date of publication, and you actually come to believe that on this one particular morning you will wake up to a phone ringing off the hook and your publisher will be so excited that they will have hired the Blue Angels precision flying team to buzz your squalid little hovel, which you will be moving out of as soon as sales of the book really take off. Or at *least* they will remember to send flowers.

I remember one year my friend Carpenter and I had books out on the same day. We talked about it all summer. We each pretended to have modest expectations. I had modest expectations for his book; he had modest expectations for mine. The week before, we talked almost every morning about how excited we were and what a long time we had waited, and how it was just like being a little kid waiting for Christmas Eve. Finally the big day arrived and I woke up happy, embarrassed in advance by all the praise and attention that would be forthcoming. I made coffee and practiced digging my toe in the dirt, and called Pammy and a few friends to let them congratulate me. Then I waited for the phone to ring. The phone did not know its part. It sat there silent as death with a head cold. By noon the noise of it not ringing began to wear badly on my nerves. Luckily, though, by noon it was time for the first beer of the day. I sat by the phone like a loyal dog, waiting for it to ring. Finally, *finally* it rang at four. I picked up the phone and heard Carpenter laughing hysterically, like some serial killer, and then *I* became hysterical, and eventually we both had to be sedated.

He sent me flowers, and before I knew he had done so, I sent him flowers, too. The ones he sent me were so beautiful, roses and irises mostly.

That is often pretty much what it is like, except for the

213

part about the roses and irises. I tell you, if what you have in mind is fame and fortune, publication is going to drive you crazy. If you are lucky, you will get a few reviews, some good, some bad, some indifferent. Don't even get me started on the places where one is neglected. There will be a few book-signing parties and maybe some readings, at one of which your publisher will spring for a twenty-pound wheel of runny Brie, and the only person who will show has lived on the street since he was twelve and even he will leave, because he hates Brie. You and the people who work at the bookstore will make lots of hilarious jokes about this. You will read to the five of them, and they will respond with great enthusiasm. Maybe there will be a couple of interviews and then probably some-where along the line, just when you thought things were settling down, your first really devastating review, the review that says your book is dog doo. It is especially festive when this review is in the local press so that all your relatives can read it, too. You can just picture several hundred thousand people perusing the review over their morning coffee, reading it out loud to one another and chuckling about how clever the reviewer is. So you rant and you cry, and then your writer friends call and commiserate. And they really do feel sick for you, and angry, and they know you feel like a wounded animal, a raging bull, and they say the right things, that they love you and they love your book, and that it has happened to them, a year ago or whenever. Because if you are a writer, it is going to happen to you. This is the truth. It has happened to me, and if you get published, it is almost certainly going to happen to you.

But the fact of publication is the acknowledgment from the community that you did your writing right. You acquire a rank that you never lose. Now you're a published writer, and you are in that rare position of getting to make a living, such as it is, doing what you love best. That knowledge does bring you a quiet joy.

But eventually you have to sit down like every other writer and face the blank page.

The beginnings of a second or third book are full of spirit and confidence because you have been published, and false starts and terror because now you have to prove yourself again. People may find out that you were a flash in the pan, that it was all beginner's luck. What I know now is that you have to wear out all that dread by writing long and hard and not stopping too often to admire yourself and your publishedness in the mirror. Sometime later you'll find yourself at work on, maybe really into, another book, and once again you figure out that the real payoff is the writing itself, that a day when you have gotten your work done is a good day, that total dedication is the point.

"When is she going to talk about *joy*?" the people in the back row whine. Haven't I? I certainly meant to mention that good hours at the desk are as wonderful as any I can imagine. But joy for me is Sam and my church and my buddies and family, and more often it is felt outdoors than at my desk.

There is a part of me that resists saying that I love being a published writer, that it has been a dream come true, first of all because it is so much more complicated than that. And second, I don't want unpublished writers to throw up their hands and say, "See? Okay? I rest my case: publishing *is* the great reward."

But the truth is that there can be a great deal of satisfaction in being a writer, in being a person who gets some work done most days, and who has been published and acknowledged. I carry this around in my pocket, touch it a number of times a day to make sure it is still there. Even though so much of my writing time is stressful and disheartening, I carry a secret sense of accomplishment around with me, like a radium pack implanted near my heart that now leaches a quiet sense of relief through my system. But you pay through the nose for this.

No one has expressed it better than a great novelist I heard once on a talk show who said something like "You want to know the price I pay for being a writer? Okay, I'll tell you. I travel by plane a great deal. And I'm usually seated next to some huge businessman who works on files or his laptop computer for a while, and then notices me and asks me what I do. And I say I'm a writer. Then there's always a terrible silence. Then he says eagerly, 'Have you written anything I might have heard of?'

"And *that's* the price I pay for being a writer."

My own version of this is that the other day, Sam and I were at the mall. I had a big event coming up onstage at the

Herbst Theater, because I had just had a book published that was getting a lot of attention. I had decided to buy a new dress for the evening. So the two of us were just innocently walking around the store when the owner came up to me. She said, "Are you looking for anything in particular?"

I said, "Well, I have a special occasion coming up, and I need a new dress."

She said, "Is it for a dinner party?"

I said, "No, actually, I'm doing something onstage."

She said, "Are you a singer?" and I felt the jungle drums start to beat, warning me to keep my mouth shut, warning me to send my ego to its room. But I had gotten used to the attention. I cleared my throat and toed the carpet and said, "No, I'm a writer."

She said, "Oh, wow! I read absolutely *every*thing. Tell me your name."

I knew I was in trouble. I knew I was going to get nailed, but my ego had become Nelson Rockefeller, and it felt like mingling. My wiser self knew I was already too far in to stop now. I said, "No, no, you won't have heard of me, and it'll make me feel terrible."

She stood firm. "Honest," she said, "I read *every*thing." Part of me believed I had become so famous that when I told her my name, she'd react as if Paul McCartney had just dropped into her store. The wiser part of me knew I was a goner for sure. I started to pray at that point, only I was praying to her: please, please don't make me tell you my name. I smiled demurely, like we'd had our fun and I'd better go get Sam, who was hiding under a rack of dresses making rude noises.

"Beth, Beth," the shop owner called out suddenly. "Come here!" A young woman stepped out from the back room with an expectant look on her face. "Beth," the owner said, "don't I read everything? Tell her!" Beth said yes, yes, this is true, she reads *every*thing. Then the owner looked at me kindly, and said, "Now come on, what's your name?"

I sighed, smiled, and finally said, "Anne Lamott." She stared at me with great concern. The room was very quiet, except for Sam under the dress rack. Then she pursed her lips and slowly shook her head. "No," she said. "I guess not."

It took me about a week and a great deal of cheap chocolate to get over that. But then I remembered that whenever the world throws rose petals at you, which thrill and seduce the ego, beware. The cosmic banana peel is suddenly going to appear underfoot to make sure you don't take it all too seriously, that you don't fill up on junk food.

All that I know about the relationship between publication and mental health was summed up in one line of the movie *Cool Runnings,* which is about the first Jamaican bobsled team. The coach is a four-hundred-pound man who had won a gold in Olympic bobsledding twenty years before but has been a complete loser ever since. The men on his team are desperate to win an Olympic medal, just as half the people in my classes are desperate to get published. But the coach says, "If you're not enough before the gold medal, you won't be enough with it." You may want to tape this to the wall near your desk.

The banana peel has appeared almost every time I've scored

a triumph, or what the world would regard as a triumph. It's God as coyote prankster. Just last week, for instance, I was participating in this illustrious literary event in San Francisco for a national charity. I had waited for years to be included in this event, each year watching six other writers be selected. I had tried to be a good sport about it, God knows I had. I understood that the organizers needed to invite big-time, nationally known writers so as to draw the biggest possible crowd; this made perfect sense. But year after year I felt dejected each time I was not included. Finally this year I was asked, and my joy was boundless. Now, I'm not stupid: I knew it was a nice big plate of cocaine for my ego. I knew it was another golden calf. But still my baby heart soared like an eagle.

However. There was this one tiny little problem. I was the last author to be asked and to commit, so I wasn't on the initial press release that went out three months ago. The publicity chairwoman sent out a second release after I came on board. But when the first big prominent mention was made in the paper a few weeks ago, my name wasn't included. I was miffed, since it was the most important column in the paper, but I am old and tough and can handle this sort of disappointment. Next there was a paragraph about the event in the book section, and once again I was not included. This time the publicity chairwoman called, upset and so full of apologies that she managed to mollify me. Then there was a big mention in the society pages, and guess what? It felt like seventh grade all over again. The publicity chairwoman called again and was so upset that I thought she might actually drink a big glass of Drano right there on the phone. I felt suddenly so teary and premenstrual and left out that I couldn't even talk about it. Hours later, I remembered that if I wasn't enough before being asked to participate in this prestigious event, then participating wasn't going to make me enough. Being enough was going to have to be an inside job.

Also, about an hour after I had slogged through to this conclusion, my mouth dropped open. I had somehow forgotten that it was a charity event! I had come to see it as a sort of showcase. For me.

Funny how that happens. I finally smiled, remembering something I heard Ram Dass say on the radio once, about somebodyism—how most of us are raised to be somebodies and what a no-win game that is to buy into, because while you may turn out to be much more somebody than somebody else, a lot of other people are going to be a lot more somebody than you. And you are going to drive yourself crazy.

One more thing about publication: when this book of mine came out, the one that did pretty well, the one that necessitated the buying of a new dress, I found myself stoned on all the attention, and then lost and derailed, needing a new fix every couple of days and otherwise going into withdrawal. My insides became completely uninhabitable, as if I'd wandered into a penny arcade with lots of bells ringing and lights flashing and lots of junk food, and I'd been there too long. I wanted peace, peace and quiet, but at the same time I didn't want to leave.

I was like one of the bad boys in "Pinocchio" who flock to the island of pleasure and grow donkey ears. I knew my soul was sick and that I needed spiritual advice, and I knew also that this advice shouldn't be terribly sophisticated. So I went to see the pastor of my son's preschool.

The pastor is about fifteen. We talked for a while. It turns out he just looks young. I said that I was all over the place, up and down, scattered, high, withdrawing, lost, and in the midst of it all trying to find some elusive sense of serenity. "The world can't give that serenity," he said. "The world can't give us peace. We can only find it in our hearts."

"I hate that," I said.

"I know. But the good news is that by the same token, the world can't take it away."

Part Five

The Last
Class

There are so many things I want to tell my students in our last class, so many things I want to remind them of. Write about your childhoods, I tell them for the umpteenth time. Write about that time in your life when you were so intensely interested in the world, when your powers of observation were at their most acute, when you felt things so deeply. Exploring and understanding your childhood will give you the ability to empathize, and that understanding and empathy will teach you to write with intelligence and insight and compassion.

Becoming a writer is about becoming conscious. When you're conscious and writing from a place of insight and simplicity and real caring about the truth, you have the ability to throw the lights on for your reader. He or she will recognize his or her life and truth in what you say, in the pictures you have painted, and this decreases the terrible sense of isolation that we have all had too much of.

Try to write in a directly emotional way, instead of being too subtle or oblique. Don't be afraid of your material or your past. Be afraid of wasting any more time obsessing about how you look and how people see you. Be afraid of not getting your writing done.

If something inside you is real, we will probably find it interesting, and it will probably be universal. So you must risk placing real emotion at the center of your work. Write straight into the emotional center of things. Write toward vulnerability. Don't worry about appearing sentimental. Worry about being unavailable; worry about being absent or fraudulent. Risk being unliked. Tell the truth as you understand it. If you're a writer, you have a moral obligation to do this. And it is a revolutionary act—truth is always subversive.

Ethan Canin insists that you should never write out of vengeance, while I tell my students that they should *always* write out of vengeance, as long as they do so nicely. If someone has crossed them, if someone has treated them too roughly, I urge them to write about it. Two of my students, in different sessions, decided to write about the switches that their parents selected from backyard trees and with which their parents used to beat them. Use these memories, I told them. They are yours. This should not have happened to you. Personally, I would write about this partly out of a longing to make sense of it all and partly out of vengeance. And this, I tell my students, may be as good a time as any to discuss libel.

Libel is defamation by written or printed word. It is knowingly, maliciously saying things about people that cast them in a false or damaging light. This means that if you lived with a man who had a number of curious personal and professional habits and circumstances that his friends and clients happen to know about, and if these friends can identify this man in your work by these habits and circumstances, you should probably change the details dramatically. If he was famous for having long toenails, make them nasal hairs instead. If he dyed his hair black, have him use foundation instead and maybe the merest hint of blusher. However, if he revealed himself through his actions toward you to be a sociopathic narcissist, you can attempt to capture his character and use actual conversations, just as long as this specific man is not identifiable by your descriptions. Change everything that would point to him specifically. Leave out his kleptomaniac leanings. Leave out the kind of car he really drove and the fact that he hated smokers so much that he planted a tiny tree in the ashtray. Make yourself the first wife or the girlfriend, instead of the third wife, and do not include his offensive children, especially the red-haired twins. If you disguise this person carefully so that he cannot be recognized by the physical or professional facts of his life, you can use him in your work. And the best advice I can give you is to give him a teenie little penis so he will be less likely to come forth.

I know this makes me sound a little angry.

I had a student whose mother, as punishment, used to burn him on the stove in the kitchen when he was little. "Use it," I told him.

"She's old, though," he said. "Her life has not been a happy one."

My heart bleeds, I told him. Change her looks, age, where you lived. If you were an only child, make up five other kids. If there were three kids in your family, have the narrator be an only child. Make her a single mother. Use the bad dad somewhere else, in another story. If there was no dad, make one up.

This guy has written some beautiful stories about his child-hood, with a mother who physically bears absolutely no re-semblance to his own. She now has blond hair and big warm brown eyes, worked at the A & P—and held her son's hand to the flame when he was naughty. One time when he finished reading, the class burst into spontaneous applause.

A friend of mine recently fell for this non-Catholic priest who seemed very learned and spiritual and tender in the beginning, and then turned out to be a mean little Napoleonic shit; not to put too fine a point on it. She wondered if she could use him as a character.

Oh, I said, I insist.

"Do I have to make him tall, so he won't sue me?"

"No, no, no," I said. Make him an uneducated writer, instead of a psychologist. Give him a past, two wives, and a number of kids he hasn't seen in years. Make him homely, make him a smoker, make him an atheist.

Give him a penis that looks like a tiny little egg in a bird's nest. He isn't going to come forward.

Maybe this is not only vengeance; maybe it is just wanting to tell the truth as it really happened. Maybe it is also about trying to find some meaning in the suffering. Well. Whatever. Here is a poem by Sharon Olds, called "I Go Back to May 1937," that I pass out to every class:

> I see them standing at the formal gates of their colleges,
> I see my father strolling out
> under the ochre sandstone arch, the
> red tiles glinting like bent
> plates of blood behind his head, I
> see my mother with a few light books at her hip
> standing at the pillar made of tiny bricks with the
> wrought-iron gate still open behind her, its
> sword-tips black in the May air,
> they are about to graduate, they are about to get married,
> they are kids, they are dumb, all they know is they are
> innocent, they would never hurt anybody.
> I want to go up to them and say Stop,
> don't do it——she's the wrong woman,
> he's the wrong man, you are going to do things
> you cannot imagine you would ever do,
> you are going to do bad things to children,

you are going to suffer in ways you never heard of,
you are going to want to die. I want to go
up to them there in the late May sunlight and say it,
her hungry pretty blank face turning to me,
her pitiful beautiful untouched body,
his arrogant handsome blind face turning to me,
his pitiful beautiful untouched body,
but I don't do it. I want to live. I
take them up like the male and female
paper dolls and bang them together
at the hips like chips of flint as if to
strike sparks from them, I say
Do what you are going to do, and I will tell about it.

I know that if you write a novel about your marriage, and your spouse is a public figure—a politician, say, or a therapist—and you say really awful inflammatory things about this person, all of which may be true, including the part about his wearing the little French maid's outfit when you made love and that awful business with the Brylcreem, you will get a visit from your publisher's lawyer, who will be very anxious and unamused. The problem is that the publishing house will be liable for millions of dollars in damages if this spouse of yours can convince a jury that he or she has been libeled. The best solution is not only to disguise and change as many characteristics as you can but also to make the fictional person a composite. Then throw in the teenie little penis and anti-Semitic leanings, and I think you'll be Okay.

◆ ◆ ◆

Try not to feel sorry for yourselves, I say, when you find the going hard and lonely. You seem to *want* to write, so write. You didn't have to sign up for this class. I didn't chase you down and drag you by the hair back to my cave. You are lucky to be one of those people who wishes to build sand castles with words, who is willing to create a place where your imagination can wander. We build this place with the sand of memories; these castles are our memories and inventiveness made tangible. So part of us believes that when the tide starts coming in, we won't really have lost anything, because actually only a symbol of it was there in the sand. Another part of us thinks we'll figure out a way to divert the ocean. This is what separates artists from ordinary people: the belief, deep in our hearts, that if we build our castles well enough, somehow the ocean won't wash them away. I think this is a wonderful kind of person to be.

Now there is only a little time left in the class, and it feels like that last half hour at camp when you've all gathered in the parking lot, waiting for your duffel bags to be loaded on the bus.

I think I've told my students every single thing I know about writing. Short assignments, shitty first drafts, one-inch picture frames, Polaroids, messes, mistakes, partners. But a lot of these people came to my class with the best ten pages they've ever written, hoping to get published, and now they wonder if this was just a pipe dream. I don't think so. Maybe most of them are not going to be published in big magazines or by big presses. They are not going to end up on talk shows and best-seller lists, are not going to be David Letterman's best friend or show Sharon Stone a good time. They are not going to buy big houses and pedigreed dogs and fish forks as a result of their writing. Many of them want these things more than anything else. They don't believe that if they got these things they'd probably end up even more mentally ill and full of stress and self-doubt than they already are. Anyway, it is not going to happen for very many of them.

I still think they should write with everything they have, daily if possible, and for the rest of their lives.

When I suggest, however, that devotion and commitment will be their own reward, that in dedication to their craft they will find solace and direction and wisdom and truth and pride, they at first look at me with great hostility. You might think that I had just offered them membership in my embroidery club. They are angry people. This is why they write.

So let me go further. There are a lot of us, some published, some not, who think the literary life is the loveliest one possible, this life of reading and writing and corresponding. We think this life is nearly ideal. It is spiritually invigorating, says a friend, who converted at eighteen from Christianity to poetry. It is intellectually quickening. One can find in writing a perfect focus for life. It offers challenge and delight and agony and commitment. We see our work as a vocation, with the potential to be as rich and enlivening as the priesthood. As a writer, one will have over the years many experiences that stimulate and nourish the spirit. These will be quiet and deep inside, however, unaccompanied by thunder or tremulous angels. My friend Tom, the gay Jesuit priest, said that he has longed for spiritual experiences all his life but that when he was drinking, he longed specifically to go into a church and have the statue of Mary wave back at him. And sometimes it did, when he was drinking—just quick little waves and then she'd sit down. But after he got sober, he could tell he'd had a genuine experience when he'd feel a sense of liberation afterward, in his chest, his lungs, his soul. This feeling is something my students report, especially those in writing groups, this feeling of liberation that, ironically, discipline brings.

Becoming a writer can also profoundly change your life as a reader. One reads with a deeper appreciation and concentration, knowing now how hard writing is, especially how hard it is to make it look effortless. You begin to read with a writer's eyes. You focus in a new way. You study how someone portrays his or her version of things in a way that is new and bold and original. You notice how a writer paints in a mesmerizing character or era for you, without your having the sense of being given a whole lot of information, and when you realize how artfully this has happened, you may actually put the book down for a moment and savor it, just taste it.

There are moments when I am writing when I think that if other people knew how I felt right now, they'd burn me at the stake for feeling so good, so full, so much intense pleasure. I pay through the nose for these moments, of course, with lots of torture and self-loathing and tedium, but when I am done for the day, I have something to show for it. When the ancient Egyptians finished building the pyramids, *they had built the pyramids.* Perhaps they are good role models: they thought they were working for God, so they worked with a sense of concentration and religious awe. (Also, my friend Carpenter tells me, they drank all day and took time off every few hours to oil each other. I believe that all my other writer friends do this, too, but they won't let me in on it.)

The society to which we belong seems to be dying or is already dead. I don't mean to sound dramatic, but clearly the dark side is rising. Things could not have been more odd and frightening in the Middle Ages. But the tradition of artists will continue no matter what form the society takes. And this is another reason to write: people need us, to mirror for them and for each other without distortion—not to look around and say, "Look at yourselves, you idiots!," but to say, "This is who we are."

In this dark and wounded society, writing can give you the pleasures of the woodpecker, of hollowing out a hole in a tree where you can build your nest and say, "This is my niche, this is where I live now, this is where I belong." And the niche may be small and dark, but at last you will finally know what you are doing. After thirty years or more of floundering around and screwing up, you will finally know, and when you get serious you will be dealing with the one thing you've been avoiding all along—your wounds. This is very painful. It stops a lot of people early on who didn't get into this for the pain.

They got into it for the money and the fame. So they either quit, or they resort to a type of writing that is sort of like candy making.

Don't underestimate this gift of finding a place in the writing world: if you really work at describing creatively on paper the truth as you understand it, as you have experienced it, with the people or material who are in you, who are asking that you help them get written, you will come to a secret feeling of honor. Being a writer is part of a noble tradition, as is being a musician—the last egalitarian and open associations. No matter what happens in terms of fame and fortune, dedication to writing is a marching-step forward from where you were before, when you didn't care about reaching out to the world, when you weren't hoping to contribute, when you were just standing there doing some job into which you had fallen.

Even if only the people in your writing group read your memoirs or stories or novel, even if you only wrote your story so that one day your children would know what life was like when you were a child and you knew the name of every dog in town—still, to have written your version is an honorable thing to have done. Against all odds, you have put it down on paper, so that it won't be lost. And who knows? Maybe what you've written will help others, will be a small part of the solution. You don't even have to know how or in what way, but if you are writing the clearest, truest words you can find and doing the best you can to understand and communicate, this will shine on paper like its own little lighthouse.

Lighthouses don't go running all over an island looking for boats to save; they just stand there shining.

You simply keep putting down one damn word after the other, as you hear them, as they come to you. You can either set brick as a laborer or as an artist. You can make the work a chore, or you can have a good time. You can do it the way you used to clear the dinner dishes when you were thirteen, or you can do it as a Japanese person would perform a tea ceremony, with a level of concentration and care in which you can lose yourself, and so in which you can find yourself.

Sometimes, no matter how screwed up things seem, I feel like we're all at a wedding. But you can't just come out and say, We're at a wedding! Have some cake! You need to create a world into which we can enter, a world where we can see this. There was an old desert dog in a comic strip yesterday, sitting with his back against a cactus, writing a letter to his brother that said, "At night the sun goes down, and the stars come out; and then in the morning the sun comes up again. It's so exciting to live in the desert." That's the wedding, right? To participate requires self-discipline and trust and courage, because this business of becoming conscious, of being a writer, is ultimately about asking yourself, as my friend Dale puts it, How alive am I willing to be?

The best thing about being an artist, instead of a madman or someone who writes letters to the editor, is that you get to engage in satisfying work. Even if you never publish a word, you have something important to pour yourself into. Your parents and grandparents will be shouting, "Don't do it, don't sit down, don't sit down!," and you'll have to do what you did as a kid—shut them out and get on with finding out about life.

Then I look into my students' faces, and they look solemnly back at me.

"So *why* does our writing matter, again?" they ask.

Because of the spirit, I say. Because of the heart. Writing and reading decrease our sense of isolation. They deepen and widen and expand our sense of life: they feed the soul. When writers make us shake our heads with the exactness of their prose and their truths, and even make us laugh about ourselves or life, our buoyancy is restored. We are given a shot at dancing with, or at least clapping along with, the absurdity of life, instead of being squashed by it over and over again. It's like singing on a boat during a terrible storm at sea. You can't stop the raging storm, but singing can change the hearts and spirits of the people who are together on that ship.

Anne Lamott was born in 1954 in San Francisco. After studying at Goucher College, she returned to the Bay Area to write. In 1980 her first novel, *Hard Laughter,* was published, followed by *Rosie* (1983), *Joe Jones* (1985), and *All New People* (1989). Her memoir, *Operating Instructions,* appeared in 1993. Her novel *Crooked Little Heart* was published in 1997. Most recently she has published another memoir, *Traveling Mercies*. A past recipient of a Guggenheim, she has been the book review columnist for *Mademoiselle* and restaurant critic for *California* magazine, and has taught writing at UC Davis and at many other writing conferences throughout the state. She lives in San Rafael, California, with her son, Sam.